Contents

Contents

PUBLIC RELATIONS

FOR

ADMINISTRATORS

By Don Bagin, Donald Ferguson, Gary Marx

Contributors include: Richard Bagin, Clem Cleveland,
Joanie Flatt, Joseph Rowson, Scott Tilden, Philip Toman,
and John Wherry

Partial funding provided by the AASA Foundation Fund.

*Published by the American Association of School
Administrators, 1801 N. Moore St., Arlington,
Virginia 22209-9988*

Other AASA publications that address effective school public relations:

Parents ... Partners in Education (booklet and video program)
Los Padres ... Participantes En La Educación
Business and Industry ... Partners in Education
Citizens and the Schools ... Partners in Education
Partnerships
Building Public Confidence in Our Schools
Holding Effective Board Meetings
Skills for Successful School Leaders
Excellence in Our Schools ... Making It Happen
Schools of the Future
Public Education ... A Sound Investment in America (video program)
The Race We Dare Not Lose (slide-tape program)
A Theme for your Schools ... Why and How
Building Morale ... Motivating Staff

Additional copies of these publications and others may be ordered from AASA Publications, 1801 N. Moore St., Arlington, Virginia 22209-9988; (703) 528-0700. Price lists and catalogs are available on request.

Public Relations for Administrators, *Copyright 1985, American Association of School Administrators, Arlington, Virginia.*

Design by Hasten and Hunt Graphic Design, Inc.

Library of Congress Number: 85-71942
ISBN: 0-87652-101-4
AASA Stock Number: 21-00146

Foreword

Take a survey of school administrators. Ask what they feel is essential to their professional success and survival. Although providing effective education for students is the bottom line, school administrators invariably and emphatically say they need to improve communication with staff and community.

Public Relations for Administrators, prepared for the American Association of School Administrators by veteran public relations professionals Don Bagin, Donald Ferguson, and Gary Marx, is a direct response to a growing demand for more effective communication, greater understanding, and increased levels of confidence in the nation's schools. This publication does not contain everything there is to know about effective public relations. It does contain a wealth of information and ideas that will help every school administrator and educator ensure more effective communication.

As you review the table of contents, you will notice that personal public relations is up front, immediately following the philosophy that supports effective public communication. Why? Institutional programs often succeed or fail as a result of the personal communications skills of individuals. Those individuals might be superintendents, members of the administrative team, board members, teachers, and others. Simply declaring a public relations program and continuing to behave in an uncommunicative manner is self-defeating.

This publication is designed to help every school leader. As you explore *Public Relations for Administrators*, you will find chapters devoted to public relations planning, internal communication, involving the community, working with government officials and the media, producing effective publications and audiovisual programs, issues management, incorporating new technology to support effective communication, marketing communication, campaigns, and evaluation.

A number of highly respected communications professionals have contributed to this important publication. Every school and school system will benefit from studying this book, discussing what it has to say with staff and community, and taking action to improve communication.

Partial funding for *Public Relations for Administrators* was provided by the AASA Foundation Fund as an indication of the association's longstanding commitment to effective school public relations. Communication is the key to understanding, and understanding is the key to support for sound education for students.

1

The Scope of

Public Relations

I still think that math program is a good one, but the staff wouldn't buy it and parents are complaining about it. I'm afraid a good program is going down the tubes because nobody feels any ownership for it.

At the board meeting last week we had a report from a task force on our grading system. During the presentation, two board members walked out to get coffee and two others were whispering to each other about another issue. What kind of impression does that leave with the community?

We announced our proposal for a bond issue last week, but now citizens are saying they can't buy the construction projects we're proposing. I don't get it. For two years, we've been telling people how great things are and downplaying our problems. Now we need help. Somehow, I think we've misread the community.

What do these three situations have in common? Each one illustrates a public relations problem. Together, they make a statement about the scope of school public relations. What caused these problems? You could conclude that in each case, either the community did not understand the school or the school did not understand the community. But if that is true, how can they come to know and understand each other? The answer to that question is a key to public relations.

Public relations plays a part in almost everything we do as individuals, organizations, and governments. Public relations extends all the way from interpersonal communication to international relations and covers a multitude of bases in between.

What is Public Relations?

Within the public relations profession, little is more in dispute than the definition of public relations. For centuries, leaders have realized that their success depended to a great extent on how well people understood

1

them and how well people perceived what they were trying to accomplish.

Some still argue that public relations is simply press agentry, which they often define as "telling people only what we want them to know." However, public relations is not a snow job. Neither is it a panacea nor a substitute for doing a good job.

What, then, is public relations? James E. Grunig and Todd Hunt, in their 1984 book, *Managing Public Relations*, say each public relations activity is part of the "management of communication between an organization and its publics." *Public Relations News*, a respected newsletter, defines it this way:

> Public relations is the management function that evaluates public attitudes, identifies policies and procedures of an individual or an organization with the public interest, and plans and executes a program of action to earn public understanding and acceptance.

The National School Public Relations Association (NSPRA) says,

> Educational public relations is a planned and systematic management function designed to help improve the programs and services of an educational organization. It relies on a comprehensive two-way communications process involving both internal and external publics, with a goal of stimulating a better understanding of the role, objectives, accomplishments, and needs of the organization. Educational public relations programs assist in interpreting public attitudes, identify and help shape policies and procedures in the public interest, and carry on involvement and information activities that earn public understanding and support.

Characteristics of an Effective Public Relations Program

Effective communication is the lifeblood of effective public relations. In fact, a sense of community inside or outside an organization results from shared information, feelings, and goals. Communication is the weave in the fabric of society, the glue that holds it together. It is the key to understanding. For anyone in a position of leadership in a democratic society, effective communication is also the key to professional survival.

The characteristics of an effective public relations program are:

- *It is planned.* In any school system, each building, each program, and the district as a whole should have a public relations plan.
- *It is systematic or continuous.* Communicating just once may not get the message across. Community demographics change daily. There are few one shot deals in effective public relations.
- *It is listening and responding.* To serve the educational needs of a community effectively, schools must understand what those needs are. Through surveys of the staff and community, advisory groups, parent groups and others, schools can identify needs, values, and expectations. Effective school community relations depends on responsiveness.
- *It is strategy development.* It is not just what we say and do, but how we say and do it. How we handle things leaves impressions about our character and competence.

Public Relations . . . A Brief History

History is filled with examples of people in positions of leadership and power who tried to impose their will on others. Some have cut themselves off from those they served and tried to rule by edict. Others have blamed the news media for calling attention to problems rather than admitting and solving those problems. And some have cut themselves off from listening to any criticism and ultimately cut themselves off from the people.

During America's industrial revolution, "robber barons" took control of many industries. One industrialist, when reminded of his public responsibility, wrote it off by declaring, "The public be damned."

In the early 1900s, news reporter Ivy Lee started giving advice to companies on how they could work better with the press. Lee declared that secrecy is the cause of suspicion. While he leaned toward publicity, he felt businesses needed to become more sensitive to the real needs of people. In 1923, Edward L. Bernays published a book, *Crystallizing Public Opinion*. Interest grew in how communication could influence public opinion. Later in the century, AT&T's Arthur W. Page declared that institutions "in a democratic country begin with public permission and exist by public approval."

Early leaders in school administration spoke of the need for effective communication as an important connection to staff and community. As schools and school systems grew in size and complexity and as communities expanded, the need for a planned public relations program also increased. School administrators began to see effective communication as basic to the legitimacy of the institution. Since the 1930s, an increasing number of school systems have employed top level public relations administrators to give leadership to this important area. The growth and the need continue.

■ *It is internal and external.* A successful organization works to communicate effectively and reach mutual understanding with both internal and external publics. Successful school administrators know that sound public relations works from the inside out. Staff members must be involved in or informed of the decisions that affect them. That maxim applies also to students, parents, nonparent taxpayers, newcomers to the community, business people, and others.

■ *It is open and honest.* If administrators are doing something that can't be discussed in the middle of Main Street, they should consider whether it ought to be done in the first place.

■ *It is essential to management.* An effective public relations program helps schools manage modifications in programs or deal with changes in public opinion. It keeps managers close to the people they serve and close to those on whom they depend to guarantee the success of the organization, administrators, board members, and staff.

■ *It involves issues management.* Through a program of listening and various other methods, organizations can spot emerging issues. Identifying, tracking, and dealing with issues early helps avoid or at least minimizes problems later on.

■ *It is personal communication.* How we speak, dress, treat others, function in a meeting, listen, handle news media interviews, are all part of personal communication, as are our nonverbal signals. Effective administrators must handle "personal" and "interpersonal" communications well.

Why Have Organized Public Relations Programs?

When school administrators are asked why their school systems have an organized communications program, these are some possible responses:
■ A public institution gains its legitimacy from communication with those it serves. Legitimacy results from keeping people informed and from listening and responding to their needs.
■ People pay for the schools with their hard-earned tax dollars. They have a right to know what they are getting for their money.
■ Any organization operates more effectively and efficiently if the right hand knows what the left hand is doing. Schools must have effective internal communication.
■ Parents, students, staff, business people, nonparents, and other important publics have ideas, concerns, and suggestions that we need to know about if we're going to be successful. By working together as a community, our schools will be more effective.

Who Is Responsible for Public Relations?

"We've hired a public relations administrator. Now that we have a professional communicator on board, we don't have to worry about public relations anymore!" Actually, just having a professional communicator does not remove the job of public relations from the rest of the staff. But it does focus on the need for good internal and external communications by all staff members and points out the district's recognition of the importance of public relations to good education. But what are the functions of the different positions?

The Public Relations Administrator: A growing number of school systems have designated their public relations directors as cabinet level administrators. These key executives report directly to the chief executive officer. They are involved in most major decisions, have access to all information, provide for communications training for staff, conduct public information and opinion research, work directly with the news media, produce publications, recommend public relations policies, and provide public relations counsel for board, administration, staff, and community groups working with the schools. They also formulate communications plans and strategies, develop systems for effective internal and external communications, form coalitions, track issues, lead campaigns, work to build public confidence in education, and develop essential communications channels and involvement activities.

While responsibilities vary from one district to another, these and other responsibilities are common to the daily work of a public relations administrator. Examples of titles are assistant or associate superintendent for communication, director of communications, director of community relations, and director of public information. Many districts have professional communicators within the public relations department who handle specific responsibilities such as editing newsletters and other publications, working with the news media and handling public information requests, directing communications research activities, working with the state legislature, or handling other needs.

If a school system does not have a public relations person, then the superintendent must serve in that capacity. Communication, a basic responsibility of all school systems, requires leadership and support from all levels. Here are just a few of the public relations responsibilities of other individuals and groups in school systems:

School Board: The board of education should establish policies that support an effective public relations effort. Budget, staff, materials, equipment, and philosophical support from the board are musts. In performing their responsibilities, everyone involved with the schools, including school boards, has an opportunity to either build or undermine public confidence in the schools and staff morale.

Superintendent: The superintendent of schools plays a primary role in effective public relations. Superintendents must often select the person who will lead the communications effort; recommend policy, staff, and financial support for the program; and perform as an important communicator for the school system. Effective superintendents support efforts to ensure that solid two-way communication exists with the board, staff, and community. They also support training programs in communication for all staff and insist that communications responsibilities appear in all job descriptions and staff evaluations. How the superintendent communicates, individually and through staff, will leave an impression about the quality of the school system and the effectiveness of school programs.

In most school systems, the superintendent does not have the time to handle all districtwide communications responsibilities. Most need a top level administrator who can provide communications leadership under the direction of the superintendent.

Central Administrators: Each school district administrator is charged with responsibility for specific programs or activities such as: personnel, staff development, elementary and/or secondary education, transportation, energy, buildings and grounds, and so on. An important part of that responsibility is to ensure that the program or activity serves the needs of the community and the staff. Departments must also communicate with each other.

Every school administrator is a public person. All are required to appear before community groups, to write and speak about their programs, and to explain their programs to the news media. Even more important, however, is ensuring that a communications component is a basic part of every area of responsibility. Communication ultimately ensures the success of these essential programs and connects them to the overall efforts of the school system.

Principals: Principals provide communications leadership for their schools. A building level communications plan should include or influence newsletters, advisory groups, parent organizations, surveys of staff and community, parent-teacher conferences, and a host of other communications functions. Every principal is challenged to get both staff and community to feel that they are contributing members of the educational

Sample Job Description—Public Relations Administrator

Title: Director of Communications

Qualifications: 1. Bachelor's and master's degrees, with one in journalism, public relations, or other area of communications.
2. Work experience in media or as a public relations professional.
3. Alternatives to above as the board finds appropriate and acceptable.

Reports to: Superintendent

Supervises: Communications staff

Job Goal: To direct the internal and external communications programs for the school system.

Performance Responsibilities:
Administration
1. Administers districtwide functions as designated by the superintendent.
2. Develops and directs a district communications program.
3. Directs the district's communications program on a local, state, and national basis, with major emphasis on local communications.
4. Serves as liaison between the press and the school system and arranges press coverage at district functions.
5. Organizes and plans regular meetings of the communications advisory groups.
6. Maintains a working relationship with community leadership and community organizations.
7. Serves as a member of the superintendent's cabinet.
8. Represents the school system at designed community, state, and national functions.

Personnel
1. Works with administrators, staff members, and community volunteers to plan and develop public relations programs and strategies.
2. Plans, develops, and maintains channels for communications with all staff.

Curriculum
1. Is well informed about school programs and activities.
2. Serves as a communications consultant for various district committees.
3. Aids in developing communications plans for curriculum adoptions.

Staff Development
1. Develops and leads communications workshops as needed and requested by the staff members.
2. Arranges development opportunities for communications staff.

Communications
1. Manages department operations with responsibility for department personnel, budget development, materials, and equipment.

Term of Employment: Twelve-month year.

Evaluation: Performance of this position will be evaluated annually in accordance with the board's policy on the evaluation of administrators.

team, as ownership flows from involvement. Principals should also ensure that staff members receive needed training in communications techniques and make communications objectives part of all job responsibilities. Ultimately, principals can be roadblocks or catalysts for effective communication.

Teachers: Each day, teachers send one thing home from school with each student: a feeling about school. Teachers play an important information role. Notes sent home to parents or personal phone calls bringing good news about student accomplishments can create a team relationship between teachers and parents that benefits the students. That team relationship is strengthened through effective communication during parent-teacher conferences. Good interpersonal and noverbal communications skills encourage parents to share information that helps teachers do more effective jobs in the classroom. Of course, what teachers say about the schools in the community is often taken as "gospel truth." Therefore, teachers must be informed about their school and the school system. Teachers deserve to be not only informed, but also involved in educational decisions. By involving staff members, schools create a sense of ownership and can use the talents of the staff better.

All School Staff: Other members of a school staff also communicate for a school and school system. Secretaries, bus drivers, custodians, maintenance people, office personnel, consultants, substitute teachers, volunteers, and all others who work in the schools are seen as primary sources of information and attitudes about school programs and the school system itself. Therefore, all personnel must be informed and involved and should list public relations among their major responsibilities.

Public Relations: A Key to Confidence

Schools have public relations whether they plan for it or not. Simply go into the community or visit with the staff and ask how they feel about the schools. Some answers may be based on misinformation or misunderstanding, but everyone will have formed an attitude. Thus, we must plan a proactive public relations program rather than wait for a reactive one to form.

No school system would think of having a math or reading program without planning for it; nor can the school buses run without a plan. But too often, communication is unplanned, and a lack of systematic communication can undermine the best educational programs for students and place school leaders at odds with staff and community.

Effective school public relations programs lead to greater understanding, support, and public confidence. The time to begin is now. This book provides basic philosophies and tested ideas for organizing or improving a public relations program.

2

Personal

Public Relations

Each day is filled with opportunities to communicate with people individually and in small and large groups. In each instance, school administrators leave lasting impressions that ultimately can make a big difference.

- Did she speak well and do her ideas make sense?
- Was his writing clear and to the point?
- Did he seem to care about my problem, and was he willing to help me solve it?
- Was she dressed appropriately?
- Does he dominate every meeting, or is he willing to listen?

Style without substance is bankrupt, but substance can be lost without the ability to communicate effectively. A philosopher once said that we make enemies in large groups whenever we make an unpopular decision, but we make friends one at a time. Making substantive, often controversial decisions can take its toll. However, leaders with good personal communications skills often can make those decisions and still be seen as caring people with conscience and integrity.

To others, our personality or ethos is a sum total of their observation and experiences in dealing with us. How do you want to be seen? How do you want others to feel about you? How do your answers to those two questions guide you in your presentations before groups, performance at board meetings, and in your nonverbal communication, dress, listening skills, and writing? This chapter takes you inside personal public relations and why it is so important. How you handle personal public relations can override everything else you do.

Interpersonal Communication

School administrators criticized for being poor communicators usually have trouble dealing directly with employees, concerned citizens, colleagues, or school board members. Why?

Many administrators tend to assume that good interpersonal communication comes from having a knack for it. They don't realize that it takes study and patience to become an effective speaker or to learn to write well. However, the same attention seldom seems to be devoted to developing interpersonal communication skills. Too many administrators are content to "wing it" in face-to-face situations, even though some of the most crucial communication takes place under those circumstances. Here are tips on how administrators can use interpersonal communication to improve public relations for themselves and their schools.

Building Interpersonal Knowledge

Probably the greatest key to good interpersonal communication is that you must care about the people with whom you associate. It is easy in any school organization to become impersonal, to begin treating principals, teachers, custodians, secretaries, parents, and business officials only as roleplayers within the organization.

To counteract that effect, remember that the people around you have families, values, hobbies, pride in accomplishments, and interest in current events. Open your conversations to these matters and encourage people to talk about themselves and things that interest them.

Learning to Listen Better

Many major corporations believe the quickest way to improve management performance is to have the managers develop better listening skills. Listening is an active process that takes skill and practice. Listening is not the same as hearing. Hearing is done with our ears only, and unless our hearing is impaired, it goes on constantly. Listening, however, is done with the mind.

Here are some factors that affect our ability to listen effectively:
- *Physiological factors.* Listening effectiveness is limited by the physical process of hearing. People can't listen unless they hear aural stimuli.
- *Processing speed.* The mind processes words faster than they can be spoken. People can be distracted easily if they aren't concentrating.

The Rigors of Public Life

School administrators are in the spotlight. Take the family out to a ballgame for the first evening of fun with the kids in months, and it's likely you'll be cornered by a parent who complains that a B + could just as easily have been an A − on his or her child's latest report card. Unless you pay attention, the parent will say you didn't care. If you pay too much attention, your family will likely say you don't care. Balancing the proper level of attention to professional, personal, and family life is a juggling act. However, some school administrators handle it very well.

For example, rather than engaging in a long discussion, the administrator might express appreciation for the parent's interest in his or her child's education and suggest a call to the teacher or principal. "I'm sure they'll be able to explain. Our family has really been looking forward to this ballgame. May the best team win. Call me at the office if you have any questions after you've talked with the principal." Reflect your obvious concern, but at the same time reflect the fact that tonight is an important night for your family to enjoy.

Listening skills, nonverbal communication, and group dynamics skills can help even in an encounter of this type.

- *Commitment.* Unless people are both emotionally and intellectually committed, they won't receive the full message.
- *Empathy.* Effective listening requires being able to put oneself in the other person's place and to feel at least partially what the other person feels.
- *Hidden messages.* People must tune in to subtle meanings and be aware of nonverbal cues to get the whole message.
- *Fear.* People who are frightened, for whatever reason, are not always capable of listening effectively.

Paraphrasing

Most interpersonal communication can be improved if we restate in our own words what we hear others say. At the end of a discussion, simply say something like this: "Let me make sure I have this straight. First, Sam is going to call each of the principals, Helen will call the board members, and Sally will get in touch with the news reporters. Right?" This ensures that all involved have decoded the information in exactly the same way.

Identifying the Problem

Psychologists speak of "ownership" of a problem. By that, they mean that a person who has negative feelings about a situation "owns" a problem. Failure to identify the ownership of a problem properly is a potential stumbling block to effective interpersonal communication.

Identification of problem ownership is not as simple as it sounds at first. It is not always clear which participant in a given situation has the problem. For example, a principal receives five phone calls from parents in a single day. Each parent complains about the poor classroom management in a certain fourth grade teacher's room. The principal, unnerved by the calls, resolves to visit with the teacher about the situation. As the principal enters the teacher's room and prepares to speak, who has the "problem"?

It is easy to assume the teacher has the problem, but, in psychological terms, the person with the negative feelings, the principal, owns the problem. For effective interpersonal communication to take place and to solve the dilemma, problem ownership must be recognized clearly.

Listening for Feelings

People don't always reveal their true feelings up front. Even though negative feelings often keep people from looking at their own problems objectively, people still keep their feelings bottled up. You can help by trying to catch some hint when people are holding back their true feelings.

Switch from listening to the content or words they are saying and listen for their feelings. Try to bring out into the open what those feelings are. If you are successful, the psychological relief people will experience in releasing negative feelings will be so positive that they often solve their own problems.

Three important points:
- Don't tell other people how they feel. Telling is parental behavior that can be interpreted as paternalism.
- Don't ask how people feel; that is too close to interrogation.
- Simply and straightforwardly tell people what you are picking up from

them. "Apparently, you're pretty frustrated," for example, or "You seem really angry about this."

The most important thing is caring. Once you have opened the door by showing you care, you can bet they will unload their true feelings and work with you toward reaching a reasonable solution. Many people simply won't let you deal with the intellectual side of a problem until they are sure you know how they feel.

Being Assertive

The two most common ways of dealing with negative feelings are to ignore the problem and hope it will go away or to "attack" the people we think are responsible, often leading to alienation and resistance.

Assertiveness is a third alternative, a middle ground between submission and aggression. Assertiveness is a four-step process in which you must:

- Explain objectively to others how you see the situation without editorializing or blaming. Also, don't assume they are already aware of the problem.
- Explain how you feel about the situation. Don't be shy, but don't over-dramatize your feelings. Tell the others involved exactly how you feel.
- Explain what you think will be the consequences if the situation is not corrected. Don't threaten and don't conjure up imaginative horrors. This helps others see that there is a problem.
- Be willing to listen to the other side of the story. Psychologically prepare yourself to listen to the perceptions and feelings of other parties involved in the situation.

Assertiveness will not solve all problems, but it will improve the odds that the problems can be resolved. It is an open, honest, clear approach—one most people can deal with much easier than they would deal with evasive and manipulative approaches.

Working in Groups

Much of a school administrator's communication time is spent in meetings. Although meetings are an important tool administrators have for getting work done, they often eat up valuable work time. It is possible, however, to maximize meetings as tools by following a few simple guidelines.

- *Decide whether a meeting is necessary*. A meeting is usually not necessary if there is no decision making involved in the issue or if you just want to pass on information.
- *Use small groups*. If the group is large, break into subgroups to take on specific tasks.
- *Draw out silent members*. Make sure they aren't withholding valuable information. Ask them for ideas and assure them that their comments will be valued.
- *Deal with conflicts directly*. Devise methods to move away from arguing the issues and toward searching for a solution. Brainstorm strategies to deal with one concise, particular issue at a time.
- *Follow the announced timelines*. Start the meeting on time and use an agenda that has the time allotted to each item marked on it. Either end on time or get the agreement of members to remain, and let those who have other plans leave without criticism. Don't make any decisions after the announced ending time. Finally, remember that two hours is the nor-

mal person's productive endurance time. If the meeting is going to last longer, build in a substantial break.

Consensus Builders Bring Out the Best in Others

In any group, there are generally four types of communicators:
- **Controlling Communicator.** Controlling communicators like to "control" the meeting and generally enter the room with their minds already made up. These people like to impose their opinions on others but aren't too keen about listening.
- **Withdrawn Communicator.** Withdrawn communicators are part of the group but hardly ever have anything to say.
- **Relinquishing Communicator.** Relinquishing communicators participate in discussions but seldom suggest action. These people will usually "just go along with Jane on this one."
- **Developmental Communicator.** Developmental communicators listen closely to the questions and concerns of everyone in the group and recommend action that incorporates the several points of view expressed in the meeting. In other words, developmental communicators try to bring the group to consensus.

Not only do developmental communicators help the group reach more acceptable decisions, they also acknowledge the important contributions of others in making their recommendations.

Nonverbal Communication

Communication studies indicate that only minor indications of a person's attitudes or feelings are revealed through words. Our words reveal the content of the message, but tone of voice, facial expressions, eye movements, and body language give cues as to how we feel about that content. There are specific types of nonverbal cues:

Spatial cues.

We must be aware of how we and other people use space to communicate. The situations in which people find themselves, the nature of the relationship, the topic of conversation, and physical restraints all help determine the appropriate distance. Categories of distance in most normal situations are:

Intimate distance	0-18 inches
Personal distance	18 inches to four feet
Social distance	four to 12 feet
Public distance	12 feet or more

Visual cues.

The face may communicate both emotional state and thought processes. Capable of more than 5,000 different expressions, faces can communicate many emotional meanings more accurately than any other factor in interpersonal communication. The face can, for example, reveal levels of interest or exhibit a level of intensity of feeling. It can communicate the

The bore and his victim

amount of control people have over their expressions and any evaluative judgments through pleasant or unpleasant expressions. It can also show whether a person understands something or not.

Studies at Yale University show that the most important thing in determining whether you impress others favorably is how often you smile. The difference between a phony smile and a sincere smile is that the sincere smile flashes repeatedly and at appropriate times, whereas a phony smile fades quickly and appears to be used to cover internal anxiety or hostility. Other studies indicate that the more we direct our faces toward the people to whom we talk, the more we convey a positive feeling to those people.

Eye contact.

The single most important facial cue is eye contact. Eye contact can be used to seek feedback from another person, to open or close communication channels, to create anxiety in another person, to show whether we feel rewarded by what we see, to indicate we are competing with another, or to indicate we have something to hide.

Body language.

The body can reinforce facial communication, particularly by indicating the intensity of an emotion. Posture can show levels of relaxation, warmth, status, inclusiveness, or deception.

For example, crossed legs or arms, clenched fists, and pointed index fingers indicate defensiveness. Pinching flesh, tugging on ears, or hiding hands in pockets sometimes indicates insecurity. Drawing back or rubbing eyes may be a sign of suspicion.

Open hands and uncrossed limbs display signs of openness and cooperation. A tilted head and chin stroking usually mean the person is in the process of evaluating what you are saying.

Gestures.

Hand gestures rank second in importance to facial cues. Gestures play a central role in interpersonal communication because they may be used

Evaluation gestures

instead of words or to reinforce verbal messages. They may also convey our level of forcefulness and energy or demonstrate our evaluation of a situation.

Vocal cues.

Our emotional state can be conveyed with vocal cues: how loudly or how quickly we speak, how much we hesitate, and how many "non-words" or meaningless phrases we insert into sentences. For example, a great variety in vocal pitch is usually perceived as meaning the person is dynamic and extroverted. Nonwords—stammering, incoherent "uhs" and "umms"—usually increase when we are nervous or ill-at-ease.

Remember, though, that interpreting nonverbal language is not a precise science. Nonverbal cues always occur in a certain context and should never be viewed in isolation. It's important that we don't misinterpret nonverbal cues in our eagerness to understand what a person means by nodding in a particular way or by standing close to us.

Avoid limiting your observations of nonverbal cues to one type only, but review all types prior to developing a response. Remember, like all other forms of communication, nonverbal communication is influenced by a number of factors, including personality traits, the pecularities of a given situation, attitudes, and cultural upbringing.

Presentation Tips

Displaying good personal public relations skills extends far beyond the time an administrator is making an actual presentation. From the time of arrival at a television studio, radio station, PTA meeting, or community building, the administrator is on stage. Rushing into a room, brushing past technical crews, making the speech, and scurrying out again with a cursory "goodbye" often makes a more lasting impression, unfortunately, than a well-prepared presentation.

Take the time to greet people warmly when you arrive. Talk casually with the hosts of the program and the crew. Show people that you wel-

Stereotyping Can Hurt You . . . And Others

What do these statements have in common?
- "We're going to have to get another girl to do this typing."
- "Administrators are men of action."
- "Let's sponsor a stag party to raise funds for the project."

They all involve sexist communication. Use it if you like, but more and more often you will be offending someone, and your remarks will hurt you.

Most organizations make a concerted effort to use both male and female pronouns in their writing. Rather than referring to everyone as "he" or "him," how about:
- Alternating the use of he and she.
- Using a combination such as "he or she" or "he/she."
- Using collective pronouns such as "they" or "them."

Doing so shows your sensitivity to making sure that both men and women get top billing.

While you're at it, be careful of stereotyping. When producing audiovisuals or illustrating a publication, avoid showing men and women in jobs that fit the antiquated male or female stereotypes. The same is true for illustrations of children. One school administrator recalls a photo on a vocational education brochure showing a boy in a football uniform and a girl with a doll. The girl is asking, "What do you want to be when you grow up?"

come their comments; doing so may even help in calming backstage jitters prior to the presentation.

Be at ease and be yourself before, during, and after the scheduled program. Practice sessions help ease tension and will help you become familiar with the text of your presentation. Knowing your subject makes it easier to relax in front of an audience.

Regardless of the medium you are using to communicate information—television, radio, or public appearances—there are a number of factors to consider when you are making a successful presentation. Of course, some points are more pertinent to one medium than another, but none should be discounted.

Be prepared.

What do you want to say and why? A good presentation is one that can be summarized beforehand. Make a mental outline of the information you want to present.

However, the presentation must be flexible. Nothing can be more unnerving than having to answer questions or discuss topics that aren't rehearsed. A good way to anticipate these questions is to try to determine beforehand the nature of the audience. How much will listeners know in advance about the topic? What are the objectives, concerns, or biases of the group you are addressing? What might they want to know, regardless of the topic?

If you are being interviewed on radio or television, watch the program in advance to learn more about the format and the interviewer. If you are making a public appearance, find out how long you will be speaking, whether a question-and-answer session will follow, and as much as possible about the group or club sponsoring and attending the program.

Listen.

Wait until you hear the full question before you start to answer. Cutting questioners off before they have finished talking not only annoys them, but it may also necessitate a follow-up because the initial question was misinterpreted. If you aren't sure what the questioner wants to know, wait until he or she has finished to ask for clarification.

Be accurate and honest.

Don't state facts and figures if you are not sure of them. If someone needs a fact or figure and you don't know it, say that you will call later and be sure to call. If you are not the right person to speak on a subject, don't. Defer to someone who is.

Be specific.

Avoid vague generalizations and be cautious about speculating on what could happen. Also, think twice before offering a personal opinion. The interviewer and audience will hear your response in reference to your official capacity. For example:

■ *Question:* "I know the board does not have an official position, but how do you personally feel, as a parent, about the proposal for a 240-day school year?" asks a reporter.

■ *Answer:* "I am sorry, but my personal position is not what we are here to discuss. The board will take action at its meeting next week. They'll ultimately determine the district's official position on the matter."

Be energetic.

Show your enthusiasm by sitting or standing straight, smiling, and looking directly at the host or person asking questions. When making the presentation, scan the audience with your eyes and talk *to* them, not *at* them. If the interview is being conducted for radio, speak in a well modulated, calm voice, but avoiding using a monotone. Inflection is important for both holding the audience's attention and stressing the important words and phrases that listeners should remember.

Build bridges.

Find opportunities to link interview questions to what you feel the audience needs to know. Don't be reluctant to take advantage of an interview or presentation opportunity to focus on points you intended to make when you accepted the interview. Plan up to four key points to make, and reinforce them. For example:

■ *Question:* "Don't you think the board made a hasty and poorly thought-out decision on attendance boundaries last week?"

■ *Answer:* "Boundary changes are difficult decisions to make, and it is easy to second-guess them. However (bridge), the board made very significant curriculum changes at the same meeting. It's important that your viewers understand the three important ways this will affect their children this fall, in addition to the attendance policy changes. I'd like to tell you a little bit about the curriculum changes, if I may."

This example illustrates how an interviewee may move into a new subject, bringing the interviewer and audience along. Bridges help to set the

Power and Using It the Right Way

"I manage a budget of $200 million. I have a staff of 12,000 people. I run the biggest business in town."

That's true in many communities. The school system, in terms of budget, number of employees, and size of physical plant, is often the biggest business in town.

Some who are bestowed with great responsibilities feel that privilege should accompany this power. However, what those privileges are should be measured against ethical conduct and behavior that is acceptable to those who live in the community.

In the worst scenario, employees are ordered to do things they feel should not be done, but do them out of fear for their jobs. Contracts are awarded without using appropriate bidding procedures. Displays of opulence exceed what is acceptable to the community. Arrogance replaces caring.

Trust wanes, gossip abounds, personalities clash, investigations begin, feelings are hurt, fear grows, relationships are destroyed.

Those in positions of power and authority should focus on their responsibility and the contribution they can make to the community they serve. Any school leader must first and last be a servant of the people.

---

tone and content of the interview. However, this technique should not be used to avoid answering questions that can be handled logically.

Be likeable.

Avoid being hostile or reactive, and try to put the audience or viewer on your side. A sense of humor is important, but don't trivialize things. If the interview is for television, don't play to the camera; professionals know how, but it can be a disaster if an amateur tries to pull it off.

Never say "no comment."

When school staff members speak on school issues, the public considers them experts. "No comment" gives the impression that you and the district have something to hide. Practice handling questions that can't be answered at the moment.

Never assume.

Don't assume your audience knows what you are discussing and that the interviewer or audience supports education. The audience sometimes will be friendly and sometimes unfriendly. If you know the presentation topic before you make the appearance, it may give you an advance clue about the audience's attitudes.

Avoid jargon.

Use terms your audience will understand and explain any new terms. Provide examples that have meaning to your audience.

Be concise.

Avoid being longwinded. Say what you have to say in a clear, conversational, and friendly manner. Spare your audience a 20-minute history when all they want to know is a single fact. Put the facts in context, but do so as concisely as possible.

Be stimulated by your audience.

Let them know in what you say and how you say it that you care about them and enjoy having the opportunity to appear before them.

Props for Presentations

Microphones can be a key to making a good presentation. If the room is large and the audience cannot hear what is being said, the message is literally lost in the process.

However, some administrators do not work with a microphone on a daily basis and may be unfamiliar with how to handle one. Every microphone is different; some are sensitive and pick up noise easily, while others may need to be held a certain distance from the mouth. If possible, arrive at the designated speaking room early and test the microphone prior to the presentation.

The same advice holds true for other equipment, including overhead, slide, and film projectors; screens; video units; lecterns; writing boards; and chairs. Tell the program host or hosts what you require for a personal appearance.

If your presentation includes "handouts," information that audience members can take with them for reference, save the materials for the end of the presentation. Effective speakers know that to get the message across, all eyes must be on them. Handing out materials detracts from the presentation, and some audience members read the materials instead of listening to you.

If the handouts contain information crucial to your presentation, use transparencies on overhead projectors, slides, or charts. This allows you to incorporate the material into your speech and to hand out the supplementary material later.

Few people know how to give an effective, concise speech without prepared notes. However, many inexperienced speakers fall into the "reading trap," gluing their eyes to their notes instead of on the audience. To avoid this, practice the speech until it becomes familiar and supplement it with a simply worded outline on numbered index cards. Index cards will also eliminate distracting noises that shuffling papers make near the microphone.

Appearance as a Factor

Personal appearance is a major determinant, in many cases, of how an audience will perceive a speaker. The first impression, although a cliché, is nevertheless crucial for speakers who wish to have a positive effect on others.

These suggestions are rules-of-thumb for television and other personal appearances.

■ *Dress in understated business attire.* Studies show that speakers are taken more seriously if they are dressed conservatively. Men should wear dark suits, solid-colored shirts, and striped or other conservative ties and longer length hose. Women should wear longer skirts and dresses. Neither men nor women should wear small, busy-print clothing of any sort.

- *Avoid distracting accessories.* This includes loose jewelry, heavy rings, and other accessories. Beware of light-sensitive glasses; television or stage lights darken them excessively.
- *Don't shirk television make-up.* Soft make-up eliminates a shiny forehead or nose under the lights. However, women should not wear bold rouge or lipstick. Muted colors will enhance but not distract.
- *Remember good posture.* Stand straight with your hands out of your pockets, and don't rock back and forth. Keep collars and ties straight and jackets pulled down around the neck and buttoned when seated for television interviews.
- *Stay informed about current styles of business dress.* Try not to wear outdated ties or suits. One or two contemporary, conservative suits should not be exhorbitant in price. Indeed, they will be a valuable investment.

Write to Communicate, Not to Impress

The way you write also may determine how successful you and your schools become. Your writing style and what you choose to say can dramatically affect many things, including staff morale, taxpayer and parent support, attitudes of critics, and the board's response to key proposals.

To write well, most school officials may have to forego the style used for a graduate thesis. Long sentences loaded with words of five syllables don't do much to build confidence. For example, compare the first paragraph of these letters sent by two principals. Each had the same intent: to encourage people to visit the schools during American Education Week.

- *Letter 1:* In keeping with the spirit of American Education Week, I am desirous of your presence in the schools any time during the week of October 19. Only when a concerned populace becomes cognizant of educational institution offerings will the potential of that institution be realized.
- *Letter 2:* Watching your boy or girl learn is something special, and we would like you to be a part of something special next week. It's American Education Week, and your visit to the classroom will help us all do what we want to do best: help your child learn better. Your child's teacher will be calling to invite you to see Brian or Lisa in action.

Which letter tells you the administrator wants parents to visit? Which one reads as if it came from the predecessor's letter file?

For some tips to help you write better, refer to the chapter on "Planning Publications." Remember that everything you write is for your audience, not the writer.

3

Planning for
Public Relations

Every school system should have a communications plan. So should every school building and every department. In fact, the communications component in all plans will force attention to the need to inform and involve those who are or will be affected by schools and school programs.

"Tell me about your public relations program." The school administrator responded, "Well, we have a newsletter, and the newspaper covers our board meetings." Both are bread and butter items. However, collectively they do not constitute a well-organized public relations plan. An effective program requires a sense of direction, a set of objectives, and strategies that involve multiple communications techniques.

The Four-Step Process

Most practitioners agree that there are four basic steps in the public relations management process. Those steps are:

■ **Research:** Knowing staff and community, understanding what people know and don't know, exploring attitudes and the depth of those attitudes, and identifying issues represent some of the types of research that contribute to effective public relations.

■ **Plan:** A plan consists of a description of how public relations is handled (the existing plan) and a road map for future communications challenges. Plans should be developed for each department or subject area, each building, and the district as a whole, and updated frequently. Questions to ask in developing a plan include: Who needs to know or understand? What do they need to understand? How will we inform or involve them?

■ **Communicate:** This step involves communication using both interpersonal and mass communication.

■ **Evaluate:** Evaluation and research enhance each other. A survey, for example, might indicate progress made in informing the community and might indicate changes in the environment that will lead to a modification in plans.

Bernays on Planning

Edward L. Bernays, father of the public relations profession, wrote *The Engineering of Consent* early in his career. The book contains one of earliest explanations of effective planning for public relations.

Bernays is quick to point out that his use of the word "engineering" should not be taken to mean "manipulation." Inspired by Thomas Jefferson's belief that the consent of the people is basic in a democratic society, he developed a process for earning support through informing, educating, and persuading.

His steps include:
- Developing concrete goals
- Gathering research
- Reorienting your goals
- Developing a strategy
- Establishing a theme
- Developing themes and appeals
- Organizing your people
- Timing and planning of tactics
- Preparing a budget.

A strategy, Bernays says, is how you are going to do something, whereas a tactic is a specific thing you will do to accomplish it.

Bernays believes strongly in seeking the ideas and support of respected people in the community. When they are involved and endorse the project, you benefit from "gilt" by association.

Research: You Have to Know the Territory

Public relations planning must begin with research. We must understand those we serve if we are to have any hope of building understanding with them and serving their needs. In other words, you have to know the territory. Here are some techniques schools use to get acquainted:
- Review the demographics of the community. Pay particular attention to age, the number of homes with students in school, the number of single parent households, socioeconomic factors, and other indicators that help describe the community.
- Study the results of past opinion polls, recent bond or finance elections, and reactions to various issues that have arisen in the community.
- Conduct surveys of the staff and community to determine what they know and don't know, what they understand and misunderstand, what their attitudes and priorities are and the depths of those attitudes, and what they feel are the greatest educational needs in the community.
- Determine who the key communicators are in your community—those who communicate with many others.
- Determine what people want to know and what they feel would be appropriate goals for education in the community.

The school system, individual school, department, or education program is connected with those affected by it through formal and informal research, surveys, meetings with advisory groups, scouring the files, and other methods. An analysis of that research builds a strong foundation for a communications plan. When top administrators and board members pay attention to their research results, they are more likely to develop policies and programs that will be acceptable to staff and community. Research also reveals information shortcomings and gives administrators a handle on how much more they have to communicate before a program will be accepted.

Plan: Key Questions to Ask

There are many ways to plan. Some prefer to take a look at where they are now and compare it with where they want to be in five years. They then develop a plan that will get them from where they are to where they want to be. Some like to dream, to put the present and past aside and to try to see things as they ought to be, and then develop a plan to reach Utopia. One method of planning focuses on informing and listening. Here are some key questions for the *informing* phase:

■ *If we're going to be successful, who needs to know or understand and who needs to be involved?* The answer to this question will help to identify important internal and external publics. If the list is long, place those publics in priority.

■ *What do they need to know if we're going to be successful?* This is the content question. Too often, a communications piece is completed, and then we discover that we didn't fully explore what people really needed and wanted to know.

■ *How will we communicate with them?* What communications channels and techniques, what involvement activities, will be most effective in helping us communicate information, ideas, and feelings to those who need to understand? Generally, the list will be long, and only the most effective approaches are selected. Often, schools already have many ongoing channels for communication that will support their efforts.

Although answering these questions generally results in a plan for telling, you can modify the process slightly to focus on the school's need to listen to its publics. Applied to *listening*, the steps become:

■ *If we're going to be successful, whose advice or support do we need? Who will be affected?*

■ *What do we need to know?* Here, we might want to know how well informed key groups are, what their attitudes might be, and what their priorities are.

■ *How will we seek their ideas, concerns, and suggestions?* Several techniques might be applied, ranging from surveys to meeting with advisory groups.

There are two important points to remember. Often, in asking people what they want to know, you will find that they want to know something other than what you have been communicating. You must also be willing to share information that is legitimate public knowledge. In addition, when asking how people feel, you may find sometimes that their attitudes are negative. Schools must be open to dealing with that information in tailoring their communications programs and must not write it off because it reflects a point of view schools don't agree with.

By knowing what our publics need and want to know, we can target our communications effort in such a way that we ultimately educate the community about the schools and the schools about the community. That form of two-way understanding is basic to a sound program.

Communicate

Step 1: Identify Internal and External Publics

As we begin our public relations planning process, we are faced with identifying individuals, groups, and organizations that must understand us or that we must understand. Identifying our internal and external publics is basic.

An *internal* public represents a group or individual having a direct relationship with the organization. The most commonly listed internal publics for schools are teachers, administrators, custodians, secretaries, bus drivers, school board members, nurses, crossing guards, food service people, central office staff, maintenance personnel, and others. Parents who are greatly involved in the school are often listed as an internal public.

An *external* public represents a group or individual having an indirect relationship with the organization, but whose actions or attitudes have an effect on what the organization hopes to accomplish. Some external publics are many parents, nonparent taxpayers, news media, the mayor, members of the city council, county board or state legislature members, vendors, business and professional groups, the PTA, fire and police departments, community service agencies, realtors, the clergy, doctors and dentists, colleges and universities, the state department of education, and others. In areas near a military base, know the commanding officer or other military-related people. In areas with large retirement communities, remember older citizens as a special public. In communities with high turnover, know your newcomers. In fact, newcomers and older citizens frequently hold an important place on the lists of communications planners.

Some schools identify lists of key communicators, those who are themselves channels for communication. These key publics might include: barbers, beauty shop operators, bartenders, cab drivers, doctors, dentists, various community leaders, and the news media.

Step 2: Determine What to Communicate

Content, the substance of communication, can be data or a feeling or attitude. Nevertheless, we must be concerned about what people need or want to know if we are to be effective communicators.

Let's say a school district is adopting a new language arts program. What do staff and community need to know about the program? First, they might want to know why it was chosen. Second, they might want to know who was involved in choosing it. Third, they might want to know how it will improve language arts skills, in other words, what they can expect in terms of student performance and when they can expect it. Fourth, they might want to know what the term "language arts" includes: creative writing, spelling, media, speaking, other items.

Let's take an important public such as the business community. What do members of the business community need to know? They need to know how they can support good education in the schools. Second, they need to understand that their future employees and future markets are in school today. Third, they need to know that the quality of life in the community depends on excellent schools. Of course, business people need to know much more.

Most schools and school systems want key publics to know their mission and goals, who the contacts are for various concerns, how effective

Writing a Public Relations Project Outline

Briefly state the project
- Coffees in parents' homes with principal, staff member, and student representatives and small groups of parents.

Purpose(s) of project
- To provide a comfortable place for parents to ask questions that concern them about the school program.
- To get feedback from parents concerning the school's programs.
- To determine communication gaps and needs.
- To test reactions of parents to new ideas.
- To explain new changes and programs.

Procedures
- Principal selects and blocks calendar dates and times, morning, afternoon, and evening.
- Principal sets up schedule of staff (student) participation.
- Parent group seeks coffee hosts and fills schedule with locations.
- Principal uses street printout of parents to guide parent group in organizing coffees (or decides to use rooms or "home base" for the invitation list for each coffee).
- Parent group calls and invites parents about one week to ten days ahead. Those who can't come are asked if they could make one of the other dates.
- Reminder notes of the coffee may be mailed four-five days before—or a short reminder call. The note is preferable.
- School representatives should be early in arriving; be punctual in ending; be prepared to offer a program if there are few or no questions. They may find it good to be able to *ask* the questions of parents to get some feedback.

Resources
- Cover for staff who attend (internal)
- Postage, first class post card per acceptance
- Printing of reminder cards 3/.01
- Mailing labels, minimum $5/run
- Coffee and cookies—PTA expense or contributed by hosts

Timing of Project
- Project will begin on (date) and run for 15 weeks.
- Schedules to be prepared by (date).

Evaluation
- Each participant will be asked to fill out an anonymous reaction form and leave it with the parent host, who will send them all to the school.

the schools are in meeting the educational needs of the community, how test scores reflect changes in the curriculum, budget needs, and a host of other important information.

Schools also want key publics to know some things that are less concrete but just as important in shaping attitudes and building understanding. For example, many schools want community and staff to realize that education is an investment, not an expense; that the future of the community is in school today; that the schools care very much about them and their children; that the schools work hard to be responsive to the educational needs of both children and adults; and that education is basic to a free and democratic society.

Step 3: Decide How We Will Communicate

After identifying publics and determining what each important public wants and needs to know, the next step is to identify channels for communication and activities for involvement.

Many professional communicators warn against overcommunicating. Our environment is cluttered with billboards, bumper stickers, promotional mail, magazines, newspapers, radio, television, information from electronic data banks, and other media. All of us have a friend who photocopies things we "should read" or passes along a book that "everyone is reading." Communicating effectively is often like finding a safe and effective way to get through a blizzard.

Various types of communication can be used in combination to communicate specific messages to specific publics. Generally, effective communications strategies involve both interpersonal and mass communications techniques.

Frequently used channels for communication include: newsletters, brochures, advisory councils, surveys, phone calls to parents, good news notes, coalitions, "coffee klatches," news releases and news reports, face-to-face meetings, open houses, having administrators teach for a day, luncheons, speakers, awards programs and ceremonies, demonstrations and displays, lobbying, and many others. Most important is that the channels selected should help get the message through.

Those who receive school communications are becoming more and more quality conscious and aware of what constitutes good and bad, appropriate and inappropriate media. Schools should communicate in such a way that they reflect good taste and sensitivity to their audience.

When methods for communication have been identified, they should be placed in priority. We may not be able to do everything. However, we must do the combination that will be most effective. For each communications activity, the following information should be spelled out:

- A description of the activity
- A list of objectives for the activity
- A list of procedures that includes who will do what by when
- A list of resources needed
- A means of measuring success.

Sample Public Relations Project Outline

Project: Principals' advisory groups will be formed in each school.

Objectives:

- To act as a sounding board for ideas, and to aid the principal in presenting educational programs to the community.
- To determine what concerns representatives of the community have. .
- To listen to the publics' questions about the schools and their programs and to use those questions to provide answers.
- To gain creative suggestions for dealing with problems or opportunities facing the school.
- To increase group members' knowledge of the school and its programs.

Procedures:

Who	Does What	By When
Principal and PTA President	Review guidelines for an advisory group and appoint seven parents, three school staff members, and two nonparents to the group.	By June 15
Principal and PTA President	Survey appointees to determine best meeting times. Set agenda; identify possible agenda items for future meetings. Distribute agendas in advance of meetings.	By August 28
School Secretary	Make calls to remind members of the meeting.	First week in September
Advisory Group	Hold first meeting	By September 10
Principal	Prepares minutes; copies to group members and district communications office.	By September 20
PTA President	Presents brief report on advisory group activities at a fall PTA meeting.	September or October

Resources Needed:

- Postage for mailing agendas, minutes
- Refreshments for meetings
- Assistance of school secretary and volunteer help
- Printing of materials
- Training to ensure productive meeting
- Information packets about the school

Evaluation:

- Ask each participant to complete an evaluation form.
- At a meeting, review accomplishments in relation to objectives.

A Workshop Can Help Build Ownership for the Plan

Many schools and school systems develop their communications plans or at least get a great deal of advice from staff and key members of the community by working through the communications process just described. When all are involved in identifying publics, determining what they need to know, and in figuring out how to reach them, they are more committed to playing their particular communications role and in making the program work. They are more likely to see that communications activities may take time but are an investment that saves time and helps avoid problems in the long run. They also understand that high quality education demands understanding and support that can only come from effective communication.

When you involve people in the planning process, let them know that status quo activities are just fine and may be working very well. However, the program might benefit from new ideas and new approaches that surface during brainstorming. Your district planners can devise ways to ensure that people have good experiences with the schools. Community education plans might extend educational programs and understanding to those who have no children in schools. Training and re-training programs offered in the schools can help businesses keep employee skills up-to-date and also make more efficient use of school buildings and produce revenue for the schools.

Don't Forget Financial Support

If planning takes place, programs are identified, and then the schools decide no funds are available to support them, not much will happen. Too often, potentially effective communications plans starve to death. Schools must provide dollars for the people and materials needed to support the program. Communications programs are not always expensive, but they do require financial support.

Allow for Formal and Informal Evaluation

Schools operate within a changing society. Volatile issues come and go. Therefore, it is not always easy to get a firm reading on changes in attitudes about schools. With those idiosyncracies in mind, schools should try, however. Attitude polls of staff and community can help identify trends and reveal areas in which further communications planning is needed. They can help reveal what works well and what might be more effective. As stated earlier, research blends with the final step, evaluation. The communications process is circular.

Other methods for evaluating communications programs include:
- Establishing and attaining objectives.
- Soliciting comments from an advisory group.
- Counting types of phone calls received.
- Actually performing communications activities.

One method to avoid in evaluating a public relations program is measuring column inches in the newspapers. If too much pressure is applied to get things in the paper, other more valuable channels could be over-looked. In some cases, communicators may become overly insistent in working to get information in the paper that editors don't consider news. In the long run, credibility with the media could suffer. The method should be tailored to the project involved and to the overall effect of the communications effort.

Building Public Confidence In Our Schools

The AASA publication *Building Public Confidence In Our Schools* suggests 12 steps schools might consider in undertaking confidence-building efforts. Each step is accompanied by a number of suggested activities. The premise is that schools must first be committed to providing a high quality product, then effectively communicating through interpersonal and mass communications techniques. The 12 steps are:

- *Strive for quality.* No matter how good the schools are, strive to make them better tomorrow.
- *Create a spirit of caring.* We must demonstrate that we care about students, staff, and community so that they will care about us.
- *Share the good news about schools.* Be honest. Let staff and community know what is working well. Also let them know what needs improvement and what is being done about it.
- *Show connections.* Help staff and community see the connection between high quality education and the quality of life in the community.
- *Work with each other, not against each other.* All staff groups in the schools should communicate with each other and work in common purpose for high quality education.
- *Get the community on the school team.* Create a team relationship with the community in support of effective schools.
- *Help people more, hassle people less.* Be sensitive to those who need help. Try not to be bureaucratic.
- *Demonstrate a sense of direction.* Let everyone know that your schools have a sense of direction—and that direction is educational excellence for students.
- *Be an educational leader in the community.* Be sure the schools are involved in every major community endeavor.
- *Create substantive themes.* Develop themes to cover substantive efforts to make education more effective. A good theme can serve as a rallying cry for staff and community.
- *Be an effective communicator.* A districtwide or buildingwide communications program will be effective only if the people involved are effective communicators themselves.
- *Have confidence in yourself.* Unless we are confident in ourselves, we will have a hard time building confidence in others.

These steps in building confidence also constitute a public relations plan aimed at improving the quality of education and building support at the same time.

Sample of a Communications Grid, Representing Some of the Publics and Channels

Some school systems use a grid or matrix to check up on which communication channels reach certain key publics. You may want to try this technique in your schools. A √ means that channel or activity reaches a specific public. A (√) indicates a possible benefit as a by-product.

Channels	Publics	Parents	Students	Teachers	Custodians	Secretaries	Nonparent taxpayers	Board of Education	News Media
Parent-Teacher Conference		√	√	√					
Surveys		√							
School Brochures		√							
News Releases—TV, Radio, Newspapers		√	√	√	√	√	√	√	√
Activity Calendar		√	√	√	√	√	√	√	√
Fact Card		√		√	√	√	√	√	√
Phone Calls to Parents		√							
Supt. Advisory Council		√	(√)					√	(√)
School Newsletters		√	√	√	√	√	√	(√)	
Open Houses		√	√	√	√	√	(√)		
Board of Education Meeting		√	(√)	√	√	√	√	√	√
Student Advisory Board			√						√

Making the Plan Effective in the Long Run

Effective communications plans should be updated and extended annually to reflect changes in the community and staff and changes in the objectives of the schools. Here are additional ways to contribute to the long term success of the communications effort:

■ Make communications objectives a required part of the objectives of every school employee.

■ Evaluate staff members, in part, on how well they communicate.

■ Develop and support districtwide, schoolwide, and programwide communications objectives.

■ Include communications responsibilities in all job descriptions.

■ Recognize people for excellence in communication.

The best communications plans should be flexible. They must change with ease to meet the challenges of our fast-moving world.

4

Feedback/

Listening

Many schools in the 1970s equated public relations with media relations, newsletters, and PTA meetings. In the 1980s a new emphasis emerged. Public relations could help build staff morale and obtain feedback from key audiences.

In fact, superintendents, when given a choice of ten public relations topics for a workshop, picked feedback and morale consistently as their two top needs.

Public relations efforts for schools were seen traditionally as a one-way process. The administrators and board disseminated information, and the staff and public received it. The school districts started to conduct surveys to find out what key audiences were thinking about the schools. The still-to-come giant step facing many districts is to use the feedback when making decisions.

Knowing what the staff and community think about important decisions is vital. Knowing what they think before decisions are made can help school officials become more effective and keep their jobs. This doesn't imply that administrators should immediately alter their convictions because of what others think and that decisions should be made based on what the masses want. They may not have the educational expertise to render the best educational decisions. It does mean, however, that educational leaders must be ready and able to explain why their recommendation or decision is better than the one the audience favors.

In the past few years a number of fundraising experts have discovered that including a questionnaire with a fundraising appeal increased contributions dramatically. Asking people their opinions about an issue makes them more responsive to the needs you feel are important. Regular scientific surveys can provide information that will keep the school system in sync with its staff and community. Surveys cost money, but they are usually worth the investment.

Many methods exist for getting feedback from the community: focus groups, individual interviews, monitoring editorials and talk shows, advisory groups, attending community meetings, regular phone calls to parents; the list goes on. As valuable as these techniques are to an effective public relations program, they do not replace the need for periodic surveys of staff and community.

Surveys

A survey of staff and community can cost $15,000 or more, or you can do something similar on a shoestring budget. The disadvantage of a "do-it-yourself" survey is that it may not be as credible to the public as a survey conducted by a qualified outside individual or firm. That is not to say schools and school systems should not conduct their own formal and informal surveys. They should, however, anticipate the quality of the data obtained and how it will be perceived.

When conducting a survey, consider these questions and steps:

- *What do we need to know?* Do you want to know what people do and don't understand? Do you want to know how they feel and the depth of their feelings? Do you want demographic information about age, location of residence, income level, whether the respondent has children in school or not, and other factors?
- *What groups or individuals will be surveyed?* Whose advice will you need? Will you survey everyone within the groups you select or develop a random or stratified sample?
- *How will the survey be conducted?* Will you conduct the survey by telephone, through personal interview, or through the mail? Will you use an outside individual or firm or conduct the survey yourself?
- *Develop and test your survey questions.* Choose words that people will understand. Be very careful not to skew the results by developing a question that contains a bias. If you want to read the feelings of various groups, you may wish to include an occasional 1 to 9 or 1 to 5 scale that allows respondents to indicate how strongly they agree or disagree with a statement. Once the survey instrument is developed, test it on a representative group to be sure it is clear and causes people to address the issues on which you want an opinion.
- *Be sure interviewers are trained,* if training is needed.
- *Decide how you will tabulate the results.* Who will tabulate the results? How do you want the results broken out? For example, would a straight comparison of those who support and those who oppose an issue be sufficient? Would you be served better by knowing how various age, ethnic, or geographical groups feel about the issue? If you want the survey to be accurate for various segments of the total group polled, then you will want to be sure your sample is large enough to make that possible.
- *How will you share results with staff and community?* Will you hold briefing sessions for the board, administrative team, teachers, and community leaders? Will you summarize results in your newsletter? Will you present and interpret the results to media representatives.

These are just a few of the steps in preparing a survey. There are others, depending on the magnitude of your study and the composition of your audience. If you don't have a background in conducting formal or informal surveys, get some help to be sure it is done correctly. If it is not done properly or if the limitations of the survey are not explained, the results can be misleading for the community, the staff, and the managers who use the information to make important decisions.

If your school system is in the middle of a crisis, and if critics are ready to zero in on any possible error or suspected bias, you might be wise to consider hiring an outside agency to develop, conduct, tabulate, and interpret the survey. Professional audience research firms can assist.

College professors or independent consultants often will provide the service. A cardinal rule is that the person or firm must be respected. Source credibility is important.

Dos and Don'ts of Surveys

Here are a few tips to consider in conducting your next survey.

Don'ts

- Don't consider a tearoff coupon in your newsletter a valid community or staff survey. The results will be limited, often with fewer than 10 percent of the audience responding. Little can be concluded from the information. However, this type of survey can provide valuable feedback from part of your audience, and your openness is often appreciated. You may even want to conduct an unscientific survey following parent-teacher conferences or during athletic events. Keep in mind that these unscientific approaches are simply opportunities for all to share thoughts and feelings.
- Don't relate sample size and the size of the community to the accuracy of your results. Accuracy does not double with doubling of a sample size. Method of selection increases accuracy.
- Don't place surveys for critical management decisions at a number of locations or distribute them at school events and draw "community-wide" conclusions from their results. For the survey to be acceptable, all community members must have an equal chance of being selected to participate. Surveys of this type demonstrate openness, but the results should not be generalized for the community.
- Don't use educational jargon in any of the questions. People can't be expected to answer questions they don't understand.
- Don't hide the results. If a survey is conducted with public funds, the results are public information. If you don't want certain findings publicized, don't ask questions that could lead to those results.

Dos

- Make sure you don't already have the information. It's time-consuming and sometimes costly to conduct surveys, especially if the desired data already exist in someone's office.
- Focus on specifics when designing the survey. Don't survey just because other schools are surveying but because you want to know what people think about particular issues.
- Select the sample properly. A valid sample must represent the larger population. It will do so if everyone in the larger population has an equal chance of being selected for the sample. Using a sample size of 400 will provide answers that can be projected to the larger population within a predictable 5 percent error. Using a sample of 200 increases the error rate to 7 percent. If you are seeking validity for various groups within the sample, the numbers may need to be adjusted upward.

How many you choose to survey depends on how precisely you want to know the temperature of the water. The Gallup Organization surveys the U.S. with a sample of 1,600 people to achieve a low error rate.

- Choose the survey method that will accomplish what you need at a price you can afford. Mail questionnaires usually produce more candor and reach groups that telephone callers and in-person interviewers can't. The response rate is considerably lower.

Some Types of Survey Methods

The telephone survey can be inexpensive and completed quickly, but it's easy for respondents to hang up. The personal interview provides the best information, but the cost and personnel training can be prohibitive. The drop-off/pick up questionnaire can be extremely effective and inexpensive if the right volunteer group gets involved.

Consider the drop off approach. Check with service organizations in the community—groups such as the Lions, Elks, Jaycees, Kiwanis, the PTA, local businesses, etc. See if one of them would take on the project of helping select the sample and dropping off and picking up the surveys.

When a service organization or other community group cooperates in this manner, everyone wins. The service group scores points with the community and in state competition, the school district gains credibility, and the public saves tax dollars. The bottom line in deciding on the best approach is ensuring the reliability and credibility of the results.

Another low-cost approach to determining community opinion on an ongoing basis is to enlist volunteer aid. Older citizens are especially helpful when conducting telephone mini-surveys. Some school districts do these surveys monthly or every couple of months. Some of the questions remain the same to chart changes in community thinking on key issues and to develop trend lines; other questions change each time.

Identify about 20 volunteers who will make ten calls each month. Invite them to a training session conducted by someone on your staff, a community volunteer with surveying experience, or a college professor who teaches opinion polling. After training the volunteers, schedule them to call each or every other month. Assign someone to meet with them to go over that month's questions and to give them the results before they are made public—after the board and staff have received them.

Some school systems identify a stratified sample that matches the composition of the community. Most are likely either to try to survey the entire universe (the group or groups being surveyed) or to conduct the survey using a random sample. Survey results can be quite accurate using a random sample, provided any person in the group has an equal chance of being selected.

Random Samples

Most firms conducting surveys try to ensure 95 percent reliability. In pulling a random sample that will result in this level of accuracy, it is necessary to:

- Determine the number of people or homes in your universe.
- Determine the number of units that must respond to give you the level of accuracy you desire. For example, one source indicates that to achieve 95 percent reliability with a universe of 10,000, a total of 370 must respond.

Therefore, every twenty-seventh person or home must be surveyed. Ten thousand divided by 370 equals approximately 27. From a table of random numbers, have someone select your first number between 1 and

27. If the number is 2, that would mean you would either select manually or with the use of your computer, people who are number 2, 29, 56, etc. on the list. The list might be a listing of parents, a residential list obtained from a city or county planning department, the phone book, or other sources.

■ If the person selected will not participate or does not answer a call, then a method must be worked out to select another person, giving all an equal chance to be selected. Often, that is done by having surveyors move up or down the list consistently to the next person or home.

Saving money on conducting a survey is counterproductive if the results are not reliable. Before deciding to conduct a survey using volunteers, get assurances that the poll can and will be conducted according to the rules. You will need sound information to make sound decisions.

Some school systems identify a stratified sample that matches the composition of the community. Others are setting up issue surveys to get an idea of how various groups feel about concerns facing the schools. (For a more complete discussion of issues management, see chapter 12.)

To get a lead on concerns that may be just over the horizon or to check on how attitudes compare with other districts, many school systems subscribe to the Educational Research Service (ERS) and regularly study information generated by state and national organizations such as AASA and printed in magazines, newsletters, or issues reports.

Key Communicators

One of the best ways to know what the community is thinking on an ongoing basis is to establish a key communicators network. This system does a variety of things for school officials at little or no cost. Key communicators:

■ Allow you to deal with sparks instead of fires

■ Provide you with an instant 24-hour communication network

■ Build confidence in school officials who are perceived to be dealing off the top of the deck

■ Identify rumors and share information with school officials quickly

■ Disseminate good news about the schools and challenges facing education in the community

■ Guarantee instant access to community opinion

■ Offer an opportunity to convert critics to supporters.

Here's how the process works. Talk with staff members and community supporters to identify people who talk to many people and who are believed. These key communicators may not appear on charts of the community's formal power structure. Often they are barbers, beauticians, bartenders, dentists, post office employees, small business owners, and gas station attendants.

After identifying people— and after starting the process with the school staff and secondary students—invite potential key communicators to one 60-minute meeting with the promise that you will not hold more meetings. This is especially appealing to busy people. In the letter of invitation explain that you are inviting a small group of citizens who communicate with many people. Explain the purpose: to communicate about the schools. Follow the letter with a phone call, and in many cases you can expect about 90 percent of those invited to attend. At the meeting of 10 to 12 people, share news about the schools and encourage questions. Explain that you would like the people attending to call when they hear rumors or when friends and neighbors post questions about the schools. Explain, too, that you would like to count on them to disseminate school news in a hurry when necessary.

Repeat the process with as many groups of 10 to 12 as you can identify. This builds a cadre of supporters in the community. Bonus: Administrators who use the system report that it saves time within a year because few rumors get out of hand.

Other Ways to Obtain Feedback

- Tap advisory committees as sources of feedback.
- Join service clubs to know how key people in the community think. Encourage staff members to join these groups and serve as listening bureaus. These can sometimes be more important than speaker's bureaus.
- Conduct a survey to determine which community organizations employees belong to. These staff members can serve as key communicators within the organization.
- Offer and publicize a hotline number for taxpayers to call to report rumors or ask questions. Make the reported information available to the superintendent and other key personnel.
- Get out of the office and listen to the community. Some administrators stand in line at supermarkets or set up a question and answer booth at shopping malls. Others ride commuter trains to visit with captive audiences. Some visit town meeting places to share a few cups of coffee and ideas.
- Call three parents and other taxpayers each week to get their views on the schools. This technique serves as a good will method, a source of information, and an early warning system.
- Keep a log of phone calls and periodically check it to find out what people are asking. Address the issues that come up most often.
- Maintain a news clip file. Monitor local and regional newspapers and radio and television stations to stay on top of what is being discussed and reported in the media.
- Conduct issue surveys prior to bond elections or school closings. Have respondents give you an indication of what might be acceptable to them and what might not, such as the wording of the issue on the ballot, the items included in a school building or closing proposal, or the improvements they would be willing to spend tax dollars to support.

School administrators need a feedback network. Administrators who fail to establish one may be headed for problems. Equating what a few colleagues and cardplaying friends think about the schools with knowing what the rest of the community thinks can delude administrators and board members into a false sense of security.

5

Internal

Communication

Question: What is the one best thing an administrator can do to improve schools? *Answer:* Communicate effectively with all staff and board members to build understanding, morale, and a sense of ownership for what the schools are trying to accomplish.

Effective internal communication is essential for any organization that wants to be at its best. Consider these facts:

■ An organization will reach its goals and objectives only if members of the staff know what those goals and objectives are and understand the role they must play in reaching them.

■ All staff members have information, skills, and ideas that can make the organization more effective.

■ A sense of ownership depends on having an opportunity to be involved in decisions that affect us.

■ Any institution operates more effectively and efficiently if the right hand knows what the left hand is doing.

■ Public relations is effective only if it works from the inside out.

Internal communication is the lifeblood of an organization. Yet, for many, planned systematic internal communication doesn't exist. Informing and listening to staff ideas are often noted as important but too often take second place. In some cases, staff members are seen not as part of a team, but as tools to get the job done. Many organizations, including schools, suffer from a lack of team spirit and low morale.

First, administrators must decide that staff members are important members of the educational team. That decision builds the foundation for a sound program of internal communication.

Second, school administrators need to understand what is important to members of the staff. Many studies show that managers feel employees are interested primarily in wages and benefits. However, studies also show that employees are interested in knowing what's going on where they work, in being told when they do a good job, and in doing interesting work. They want to be treated as colleagues in an important enterprise. Organizational communications expert Roger D'Aprix makes it clear that employees generally want to be treated as colleagues, not as subjects.

Third, staff members need to know what is expected of them. They want to know how they will be evaluated. Employees also want to know about any problems facing the organization and what is being done about them. In other words, they want to know where they and the organization stand.

Fourth, opportunities must be provided for staff members to ask questions, share suggestions, and express concerns in a nonthreatening atmosphere. When employees feel their voices are heard and conclude that their ideas count, they are much more likely to exhibit higher morale, feel they are a part of the team, provide accurate information for others, and become more productive in their work.

How serious is the need to improve internal communication and build staff morale? One study has shown that 90 percent of the teachers who lost their jobs to declining enrollment say they would not return to their positions. The reason: lack of feedback from their bosses. These former teachers found that their supervisors in noneducational positions let them know more often when they were doing a good job and that they were appreciated. Money was not given as a main reason for not returning to the classroom. Another alarming statistic: Only 20 percent of teachers and principals surveyed in 1979-1984 studies said they would bother suggesting an idea to improve the schools, even if their ideas cost nothing to implement.

This chapter contains suggestions for improving internal communication. In developing a plan for improving internal communication, keep in mind certain organizational realities:

■ Many organizations suffer from a "hierarchy gap," according to Michael Cooper. Managers often feel more satisfaction in their jobs than hourly or clerical workers.

■ Actions speak louder than words.

■ Employees do not identify their interests automatically with the interests of the organization. Loyalty must be earned.

■ Employees have multiple sources of information; management is only one of them. The source of information they trust most is their own experience.

■ Don't ask people their opinions and suggestions if you don't intend to use them.

■ If staff members are upset about how they are treated, they will often find a way to express their feelings in a way that is negative for the organization.*

How Can We Improve Internal Communication?

What can be done to improve internal communication and staff morale? Which communications techniques help bring about a spirit that makes people feel good about going to work, a spirit that nurtures developing ideas that lead to better education? Here are some ideas schools are using; some might work for you, and most are easy to initiate. At a low cost and with a high return, they generally fall into the areas of improving interpersonal communications and improving the quality of working relationships.

*Summarized from Communicating for Productivity by Roger D'Aprix, published by Harper and Row, 1982.

Informing, Involving, and Caring

The essence of promoting healthy interpersonal relationships is a caring approach. Insist that your schools pay attention to school climate. If staff members have lost their enthusiasm and feel they are simply cogs in a bureaucratic wheel, school climate is not what it should be. Various instruments have been developed to measure school climate, such as the CFK/PDK materials, published by Phi Delta Kappa, "School Climate Improvement: A Challenge to the School Administrator." Among staff needs are: physiological needs, such as heat and light; safety needs, such as security against abuse or assault; acceptance or friendship needs; achievement and recognition needs; and the need to maximize one's potential.

Employees need to know the organizational mission, goals, and objectives. As much as possible, involve staff members in developing objectives, formulating job descriptions, developing policy changes, and planning a system for evaluation. Help them feel ownership for the organization and what it is trying to accomplish.

Keep students informed and involved, too. Students should be among the first to know about proposed changes because they are the focus of all that schools do. In developing a communications plan, their needs for information should be met. If possible, consult students when decisions are being made that affect them.

Conduct regular surveys of staff to determine their information needs. Find out what bothers them most and gets in the way of their productivity. One business asks its employees, "What makes your job hard?" Then they develop a plan to provide information or strategies and help solve employee-identified problems.

Promote teamwork. Many companies, based on a synergistic philosophy, use quality circles, inviting the groups of employees who deal directly with a problem to explore the problem and propose solutions. Some schools use the 1-3-6 method to involve staff members in problem solving or sharing ideas. For example, seated in groups of six, participants are asked to identify one idea each that seems to work well. Then each person works with two others in the group to agree on one best idea.

Next, the two groups select one of the ideas for presentation to all. This approach helps create a spirit of sharing. If problems are identified in this type of setting, ask each group to define indications of problems and suggestions for solving them.

Develop an "I-have-an-idea" card and distribute it to all the employees. Encourage them to submit ideas directly to their supervisors or others in the organization. You may wish to require that the person receiving the idea respond within ten days or so whether the idea can be used or not. While some managers might be threatened by this approach, perhaps one copy of the idea could go to an idea mover, who would give the supervisor a call if the employee has not received a response. This process turns idea blockers into idea movers.

Many organizations also provide substantive professional development opportunities. To be effective, it's a good idea to ask the employees what they feel they need to know to improve their performances. Hold the sessions in an attractive, comfortable environment and provide knowledgeable presenters. Some staff members might serve on the workshop faculty. Provide additional opportunities for involvement in professional

Primary Sources of Information

As a school leader, you might be interested in some research done by Opinion Research Corporation to determine where various groups want to get their information. Among managers, 84 percent said they preferred to get their information from immediate supervisors. Only 5 percent preferred the grapevine. Among professional employees, 78 percent preferred to get their information from immediate supervisors. Only 9 percent preferred the grapevine. Results for clerical and hourly workers were quite similar. In other words, staff members look to the administrator for information. A prime administrative responsibility is to provide it.

organization and participation in outside professional conferences and workshops.

Other ideas for improving the overall relationships in an organization are:

■ Form a staff advisory group with a rotating membership, making it possible for as many employees as possible to meet with you personally or in a small group during the year.

■ Start a wellness program. Recognize the stress that an organization can generate and how it can affect staff. Involve staff in organizing the program.

■ Publish a staff newsletter, or if you already have one, see how it can be improved. Share information that is vital to staff members to do their jobs. Carry information that will build a better understanding of all school programs. Highlight individual staff members, schools, and departments. A good newsletter can build a strong sense of community. Ask for staff reporters in each building and department to report news for the newsletter.

■ Protect your staff members from information overload. Support them when they need help. Piles of daily mail and a constantly ringing phone can sap the morale from the most enthusiastic staff member.

■ Remember—nonverbal communication signals employees about your feelings. Nonverbally, through your facial expression and the way you walk through the building, as well as the tone of your voice, you help to set an attitude. The old adage—actions speak louder than words—continues to be true.

■ Avoid killer phrases. Nothing dampens a person's willingness to share ideas or help solve a problem more than being told: "The board won't buy it;" "We tried that once and it didn't work;" "This is idiotic;" and of course, don't overlook the ever-popular killer words, "Yes, but. . . ."

■ If changes are coming, let the staff know in advance and explain the reasons for the changes. Be clear about any impact those changes might have on employees. Otherwise, undue stress might result. Keep in mind that the status quo is often comfortable, and change is not always easy.

■ Know who feeds the grapevine and ensure that factual information is flowing through it, rather than rumor.

Some Personnel Evaluation Tips

All evaluators must overcome the desire to be considered nice people who say nice things about everyone. They must be able to point out strengths and to help overcome weaknesses. Courses in supervision and evaluation should prepare school officials for this responsibility.

The challenge often comes, however, when the evaluation results must be communicated. Many teachers feel that supervisors and administrators often discuss evaluations in a condescending tone and write in a pompous, bureaucratic fashion that allows all kinds of interpretation for what is said.

This is not to imply that teachers are opposed to evaluation. One Columbia University study showed that teachers who had moved to jobs in industry listed receiving more feedback from their bosses as a plus in their new jobs.

Perhaps the best advice is to use the kind of language, tone, and specifics that you would want used to evaluate you. Remmber that the goal is to improve an individual's performance, not to chastise.

Conducting Good Meetings

Another area that controls the way employees feel about their organization is the tone of meetings they might be attending. Here are some guidelines for conducting good meetings:

■ Make sure your meetings are productive. Nonproductive meetings send a subtle message to people that you don't think their time is valuable. Structure meetings to get the most done in the shortest time possible. Prepare an agenda; avoid rambling. Let people know how the meeting helped and how ideas were used. If a meeting is not needed, don't hold it.

■ Hold occasional "family meetings" involving all who work at the school. Share valuable information and ask all staff members for ideas and advice.

■ Set up monthly luncheon meetings with top teachers or other employee association leaders to discuss education in the school or district and to explore concerns. Many big problems can be solved when they are small if they are only identified.

Improving One-on-One Relationships

So far we have discussed techniques for dealing with groups in an organization, but here are some guidelines for improving one-on-one relationships:

■ Be available. Time management experts often discourage an open door policy that is too open, but if staff members find it next to impossible or intimidating to visit with you, communication will break down.

■ Praise individual employees for a job well done. Recognize good performance and service with notes of appreciation and other techniques. Give credit when things work; know as many names as possible.

■ Work closely with secretaries. Let your secretary know where you will be when and what your priorities are.

■ Listen to staff members who talk with you. Use active listening techniques. Ask thoughtful, clarifying questions and paraphrase what you've heard. Not only will you reassure employees that you are listening, but you will undoubtedly receive information that could improve school operations. Also encourage staff members to ask you questions to be sure they understand.

■ Remember that an evaluation is a communications process. Meet one on one with staff members. Have them comment on what is working well and on any obstacles they face. Listen to what they would like to accomplish and help them develop objectives, explaining what you can do to help them. Ask if there are times when you unintentionally hinder rather than help them. Share your goals and objectives for the coming year and ask their help and suggestions. One warning: Never penalize a staff member for answering questions honestly or for giving advice you might not like. Communication breaks down when penalties are imposed for honesty.

■ When a reprimand is necessary, be sure you have the facts and not hearsay. Be specific and avoid general complaints and unrelated concerns. Listen to the staff member's side of the story before taking action. Don't allow a reprimand to trigger a long term grudge or general breakdown in communication.

Remember, most of all, that internal communication is for everyone, not just one group. All employees must feel they are important members of the educational team.

6

The Public Relations
Role of All Employees

Your board policy handbook will usually assign the primary responsibility for public relations to a top level administrator or public relations director, but public relations policy doesn't stop there. Public relations responsibilities should be written into every employee's job description. School districts should also provide training for all employees so that they have the skills and resources necessary to fulfill this portion of their job descriptions.

Here's an example of what can happen if this is not a priority:

There's a story told about a Kansas school district and the new reading program that was introduced in the primary grades. The program, adopted after months of study, was designed to provide individual attention for students in their early years.

Unfortunately, word spread throughout the community that the reading program at ABC Elementary School was no good. The rumor persisted; so, the public relations director drove out to the school to investigate for himself.

The first person he saw upon arriving at the campus was Henry the custodian. Knowing that custodians and secretaries are the real "key communicators" at most elementary schools, the director, after exchanging greetings, asked Henry about the new primary reading program.

"It's terrible," was Henry's reply. "It's just a crying shame what those children are being exposed to."

To support his contention, Henry took the public relations director to one of the second grade classrooms, where the door was open and they could observe firsthand the learning that was, or was not, taking place inside.

The children were organized in small groups around the room, with each group obviously working on something different. There was a low hum, or buzz, in the room, as the children pursued their reading lessons enthusiastically. The teacher moved from group to group, as did a teacher's aide.

"See there," exclaimed Henry. "See all that chaos! Those kids sprawled all over the room, everybody doing their own thing. How can they possibly be learning anything, especially something as important as reading?"

The public relations director found the source of his rumor. When

45

Henry went to church, to the Friday night football games and the neighborhood pub, people asked him about the new reading program. After all, they reasoned, Henry worked there. He'd know the story .

The only problem was that the teachers and the principal hadn't bothered to tell the nonteaching staff about the new reading program when they introduced it, since these staff were noncertified people. "Why did they need to know about the curriculum?" was the rationale.

The answer is, of course, that they need to know a lot. In fact, they must be kept informed about everything that's going on at school. If there are district office employees, they must know about what's happening districtwide. If they are school-based staff, they must know about their own school as well as the major activities in the district.

That doesn't mean we tell them just the good news, the successes, the things about which we are most proud. If there are problems, those need to be shared, too, along with information on what the school or district is doing to help solve the problems.

This is what we mean by giving employees some of the tools they need to fulfill their public relations responsibilities. There are other tools.

In a large Arizona school district, all new staff members attend a half-hour public relations inservice program as part of their new employee orientation. Taught by the public relations director, the inservice session covers:

■ How to get stories into the staff newsletter
■ How to use a tip sheet to suggest stories for news media coverage
■ What a "Happy Gram" is and how to use it
■ What the communications responsibilities of staff members are
■ Suggestions for ways employees can incorporate public relations into their jobs
■ Extensive background information on the demographics of the school district and its philosophies
■ Ways the school district helps support the public relations activities of the employees
■ Channels of communication in the district and how to use them most effectively.

All new employees—teachers, principals, bus drivers, assistant superintendents, custodians, maintenance workers, aides and cafeteria staff—attend this orientation to public relations. The result is better communications throughout the district from the time employees first join the district team.

The Communications Hub

Some principals are still discovering that the communications hub of any school is the secretary. They sometimes forget that if parents have a question about school, they talk first to the secretary when visiting the school or calling on the phone.

Students who have questions go to the office, and who do they approach first? Usually, the secretary. When teachers stop by the office to check their mail, arrange their schedules or order their supplies, it is the secretary, not the principal, to whom they address the majority of their day-to-day questions.

But when it comes time for staff or faculty meetings, who is left in the office to answer the phones? Unfortunately, in too many buildings, this

Suggested Guidelines for
Public Relations for School Board Members

- We will identify the function of public relations, the district's responsibilities, and the public's right to know in our policy manual.
- We will make sure that public relations functions are in all employee job descriptions. Primary responsibility will be assigned to the public relations director.
- We will include communications goals and objectives in the district's and board's annual goals and objectives, and we will hold ourselves accountable for measuring the results.
- We will hold training sessions to improve board and board member communication skills.
- We will provide adequate budget support for public relations.
- We will make sure that communications goals and objectives are included in the annual goals and objectives for all schools, departments, and administrators.
- We will make sure that a communication component is included in every new program that is proposed for adoption.
- We will encourage feedback through surveys, advisory committees and other methods of listening on an annual basis.
- We will serve as members of the board team, rather than single-issue members.
- We will never knowingly embarrass or demean members of our staff in private or in public meetings.
- We will serve the best interests of all the students whose education has been entrusted to our care and leadership.

task continues to be given to the secretary, the one person, next to the principal, with whom it is important that all information be shared.

School board members and administrators can take the lead in making sure that public relations is an integral part of everybody's job. They can lead by example.

Many school boards have set aside a single study session to outline the public relations role of school board members (see the suggested guidelines for school board members).

Administrators can do the same thing. Starting with the superintendent, administrators include among their objectives for the year specific items that relate to communication. Staff input and suggestions for these objectives can be solicited, and administrative objectives in turn can be shared with the rest of the staff.

The rest of the staff should be encouraged to do the same. Here are some examples of public relations activities that could be adopted by various groups of employees.

Public Relations for Teachers

- *Make a pledge to send home a "Happy Gram" or "Good News Note" with one student each day, with the larger objective that each student in your class or classes receives at least one of these notes from you each semester.*

Teachers who use these Happy Grams often have fewer discipline problems in their classes for many reasons.

Students enjoy being recognized for doing something right. Parents appreciate it, too. This kind of goal each semester also focuses teacher attention on the good things that students do. Even the student with problems does something good during the year that the teacher can recognize.

■ *Make one positive phone call to a parent each week.*

Too often, the only time we have personal contact with parents outside of formal conference time is when we convey bad news. Johnny didn't do his homework. Jane is failing math. Sam was fighting on the playground today.

How about turning that around? It's a pleasure having Sue in class. She's such a hard worker. Benjamin is really trying hard. I thought you'd want to know. Is there anything I should know about Enrico that will help me help him learn better?

■ *Send parents outlines of what you're going to be covering in class.*

We talk about a partnership between home and school, but how good a partnership is it if only one-half knows what's going on? We can't always depend on students to do our communicating for us.

"What did you do at school today?" "Nuthin." That is not a productive conversation.

Parents would rather say, "I see by the schedule you studied about Abraham Lincoln this week. Why do you think he's considered one of our finest presidents?"

■ *At the end of the day, before students go home, summarize what you've covered that day.*

Students will remember what teachers highlight for them even if they only summarize all the day's activities. The technique is very effective for elementary teachers; however, high school teachers can also use it by summarizing at the end of the each class period.

Some teachers might protest that they do not have time for these activities. Administrators need to help teachers understand that effective communication procedures will save time over the long haul.

Public Relations for Secretaries

■ *Remember, you represent the school when you pick up the telephone.*

The only contacts some of our publics have with the schools and districts are by phone. How the phone is answered, including the tone of voice, the words spoken, and the courtesy extended to the caller, often make the difference between positive and negative images of our institutions. Administrators should give specific instructions about how the phone should be answered and how calls should be handled.

■ *Even when you're having an especially tough day, put a smile on your face before answering the phone.*

As silly as it sounds, it works. Your voice can't have a negative quality to it when your lips are turned into a smile. It has something to do with placement of the lips, teeth, and tongue, and their effect on voice tone.

■ *Remember that people, not paperwork, come first if you have a school secretary's job.*

Despite all the attention paid to tests and homework, education is a people business. Everyone in the business must remember that.

When students, teachers, vendors, or parents walk into a school office, they should be greeted within the first five seconds that they enter the room or approach the desk or counter. Even if you're on the phone and can only manage a friendly wave of your hand, this at least acknowledges your visitors and lets them know you will attend to their needs rapidly.

- *A couple of times each year, ask the people with whom you work how you can improve.*

Soliciting feedback results in three things: (1) your fellow workers' appreciation for the fact that you really do want to do a good job; (2) some unexpected kudos for a job already well done; and (3) some constructive suggestions on how you can improve.

Public Relations for Custodians

- *When you see something interesting in a classroom, make a point to ask the teacher about its educational significance.*

Custodians are in and out of the classrooms all the time, but seldom when the children are participating in the education process. If you see an interesting bulletin board or project in process, make a note to ask the teacher what the students are studying and how this project helps them learn better. This gives you a better understanding of what's happening in class and helps you share the information with others.

- *Make an effort to get to know students' names so that you can greet them when you see them at or away from school.*

In most schools, students seem to have a natural affinity for the custodian, and the custodian can help make school a pleasant or comfortable place to be by greeting them by name and giving them a friendly smile.

- *Work with the student government group to improve the appearance of the campus.*

Students want to go to a school that looks nice. Although it is primarily the custodian's job to keep the school looking good, good schoolkeeping is part of everyone's job. Custodians can badger everyone about picking up papers and tidying up around school, or they can solicit the involvement of students through an all-school beautification program.

- *Take a good look at your school building and let your principal know where better and friendlier signs could be placed.*

Custodians probably see more of the school than anyone else. Attentive custodians can take note of where old signs should be replaced and where current signs can be improved or made more friendly.

Public Relations for Cafeteria/Food Services Staff

- *Work with a student committee to help plan menus or special services in your cafeteria.*

One cafeteria staff did this and learned that the students were diet conscious and interested in starting a salad bar. Many people took advantage of it. Another school used the same technique and started a hamburger, fries, and shake line.

- *Plan special activities around special holidays.*

By spicing up students' daily trips to the cafeteria and making it a fun experience, cafeteria workers have learned they have less food thrown away and fewer discipline problems. In addition to adding an element of cheerfulness, they have thrown in surprises, such as costumes and prizes for best behaved or clean-plate club kids. This type of atmosphere makes going to work pleasant, and students enjoy the cafeteria more.

■ *Work with teachers and student leaders to set up a restaurant environment in one part of the cafeteria.*

For example, here is a workable approach for younger students. In one corner of the cafeteria, set up a few tables with seating for four to six at each. Set them with silverware, napkins, and flowers. Let classes take turns eating there during the year. Teachers could have a unit on table manners prior to their class's time. You might even consider serving the food family-style instead of cafeteria style.

■ *Try to reward students for their good behavior in the cafeteria more than you discipline them for inappropriate behavior.*

Whether it's buttons, stickers, extra dessert, or special privileges, your staff could come up with positive ways to let students know you appreciate their good behavior. Pretty soon you'll have everyone competing for the good strokes.

Holding Workshops for All Staff

These are only a few of the public relations ideas that can be used by different employees in your school or district. Don't forget to involve other groups, such as bus drivers, in your public relations programs.

One of the best ways to develop public relations for the people on your staff is to set aside some time for an inservice workshop on communication. In the process of determining internal and external publics and programs to reach them, you can also have staff members brainstorm their own ideas for improved public relations. Bring a group of principals, bus drivers, secretaries, or others together. They'll come up with more good ideas for their own public relations job descriptions than any book could offer.

It's important to remember that the process itself is two-way and should incorporate feedback. Public relations that involves all employees only works when there is upward, downward, and horizontal communication. That kind of communication doesn't take place without solid planning and an expectation that everyone will participate.

7

Community

Involvement

Community involvement in the schools is center stage for many reasons.

First, there may have been a time when most adults in a community were parents, but that's not so today. In fact, only 25 to 30 percent of U.S. households have school-aged children. Of course, percentages vary from one community to another. Second, we live in a democratic society, which makes involvement by various groups in their institutions essential.

Just as important as these two factors is the research that tells us people's attitudes are based primarily on their personal experiences. Attitudes drive behavior. With the growing number of nonparent taxpayers in our communities, fewer people are having direct personal experiences with schools. Therefore, astute educational leaders are creating opportunities for people from all segments of the community to become involved in their schools.

Parent Involvement

Schools deal with two things most important to many people: their children and their tax dollars. Thus, what schools do and how well they do it are of natural interest to many publics, especially parents.

Parent involvement in the schools, which is often highly visible, is essential. Many parents participate through the PTA, volunteer programs, advisory councils and other organizations. Schools generally encourage parents to take an active interest and to work with the schools to help students achieve.

Parents' interest in the schools should not be taken for granted. The schools must communicate with parents and let them know what they can do to support education.

But the challenge of communicating effectively with parents has grown complex. For example, the number of families in which both parents work and the number of single parent families have grown. Schools that once depended on parents to provide volunteer help are now finding that many graduate volunteers move into paying jobs. Not only does this affect availability of volunteers, but it also means that parent-teacher conferences and other significant meetings may have to be scheduled at more convenient times for parents, even though those times may be less convenient for school staff members.

To maintain a strong partnership between parents and the schools, schools must keep parents informed about and active in educating their children. Here are some suggestions for building this partnership:

■ Publish a regular newsletter for parents (This same newsletter could also be mailed to the total community three or four times a year.)

■ Encourage involvement through parent organizations and advisory groups. Provide leadership training. Offer opportunities for parents to comment on school programs, and use those comments to fill information gaps or to correct problems.

■ Encourage school staff members to make a phone call a week to a parent. Let parents know you appreciate having their children in school and ask how things are going. These calls can build good will and provide valuable insights on how programs are working.

■ Survey parents to determine what they like, dislike, misunderstand, and how deeply they feel about certain issues. Consider their comments carefully when setting priorities.

■ Encourage teachers to use "Happiness Notes" or "Good News Notes" to let parents know some personal, positive news about student's performance or behavior in school.

■ Let parents know what the rules of discipline are and what penalties can be expected from various infractions.

■ Provide staff training for effective parent-teacher conferencing. Conferences must be two-way, open, honest, and constructive. Some schools conclude each conference with the development of a teacher-parent plan of action.

■ Avoid ridiculing or criticizing parents who have concerns and who express them. That approach causes resentment and stifles effective communication.

Nonparents: A Varied Group

Nonparents are a less obvious but important group that must be involved in the schools. This group comprises a number of publics. Some nonparents are married adults who do not have children; others are single adults or married couples who have children not yet in school; still others are adults who have already raised their families.

But nonparents have one thing in common—they pay taxes, a big chunk of which goes to support schools. The challenge for schools is to devise ways to involve nonparents so that they will reflect a positive—or at least an understanding—attitude about the schools.

Consider, for example, older citizens, one of the fastest growing segments of the American population. Not only are they growing in numbers, but they're also growing in sophistication and abilities. They have a great deal to contribute, and although many must retire at a certain age, their desire and ability to contribute often continues.

How can educators benefit from this situation and what can they do in turn for older citizens? Many school districts and schools have already begun to tap this resource with programs in which they:

■ Invite older citizens to serve as volunteers. Many retired people would welcome the opportunity to take on significant school projects.

■ Use them as resource people. Their knowledge, experience, and expertise can be helpful to teachers, administrators, and students. Consider inviting them to be resource speakers in science, math, history, geography, home economics, industrial arts, and other classes.

■ Ask them to consider signing up as tutors. In addition to assisting in regular tutorial programs, they could be an invaluable resource in homebound study programs.

■ Use their services to conduct your surveys of public attitudes. People who are not tied to nine-to-five work routines can provide significant help.

Community education is a natural avenue when we are asked what schools can do for senior citizens. Identify this important public in your community and involve them in schools, and at the same time, you will be answering their needs.

Community Leaders

Don't be lulled into thinking that community leaders and the business community are synonymous. You have to be able to identify your community leaders before you can work constructively with them. Each community is unique, and the segments of the community from which the leaders are drawn will differ.

Here are a few suggestions that can help you identify community leaders from three levels of leadership:

Visible leaders

These are the leaders you can identify most easily. They include the people who are always on committees and advisory councils, elected leaders, fundraising leaders, and the like.

Invisible leaders

These leaders are tougher to identify. They either have a large financial interest in the community, or they have emerged as the leaders of a significant group within the political process. They are the names behind the names, and they're often selective in the use of their names for various causes. They don't always run for political office but are often involved in getting others elected.

Emerging leaders

These are the men and women who will take over the reins when current city and county leaders complete their terms of power. Many communities are actively seeking, training, and mentoring emerging leaders, knowing that this investment today will result in a better community tomorrow.

The late George Gallup said that educators should endeavor to be the intellectual leaders of the community. When people think of learning, they should think of people in the schools. Educators should identify the community leaders and make sure that they work with them in many ways. Get involved in the Chamber of Commerce; volunteer for charitable campaigns. Serve on various boards and commissions, and be active in the political process. Make it clear how the school can contribute to community betterment and how the schools will be affected by proposed changes.

When the time comes that you need to turn to community leaders on behalf of the students in your schools, you should be able to meet with them as colleagues, not as strangers.

Business Community

"Long-term economic growth is tied directly to the performance of public education." That comment was made by Richard L. Lesher, president of the Chamber of Commerce of the United States, in a 1985 report titled *Business and Education: Partners for the Future.* Never before has the American business community expressed such a deep interest in education. Business people are realizing that a sound system of education is essential to a sound economy and the overall quality of life in their communities. Many are demonstrating a desire to form partnerships.

Those partnerships must be carefully designed and expectations mapped out for both the schools and the businesses involved. Otherwise, frustration and even bad feelings can result.

An effective public relations program brings representatives of schools and businesses together to explore their common desire for high quality education. The partnership must go beyond big business simply because most communities are made up of small businesses. In fact, 90 percent of all businesses in the nation have fewer than 50 employees. Whatever business's size, it depends on schools to provide well educated, dependable employees. Many businesses also realize that well-educated people provide a better market for their products and services.

School administrators are the key people in establishing sound school/ business partnerships. Granted, they should protect schools from businesses that simply want to exploit the schools, but they should not use that protection as an excuse for not developing cooperative efforts that work.

Understanding Business Perspectives

Business people are accustomed to working with the bottom line. They relate to sound business practices, wise investments, and profit-and-loss statements. They seldom relate to "can't do" and "can't measure" explanations.

What you can you do for business? What can business do for you?

Start by determining what your community's business people expect from their schools. When was the last time you surveyed the businesses in your area? Do you know their perceptions of your schools' strengths and weaknesses? Do you know what skills graduating students will need for the jobs available today?

There are a number of ways schools and businesses are collaborating to meet each other's needs. Major corporations are loaning executives to schools, sometimes for as long as one year. These loaned executives assist educators in everything from analyzing business and personnel practices to serving as resource people in the classrooms. They are also helping educators design curricula that will prepare students for work. Adopt-a-School is a popular program in which businesses, service clubs, and professional groups assist schools through financial, material, and human resource support. This program has been successful in many school districts. Administrators should be careful to establish a partnership agreement that identifies expectations up front.

The business community is another significant nonparent public that can benefit from the services of a community education, adult education, or retraining program in your district. What can you do for them? Invite them to survey their managers and employees about the types of additional training or lifestyle classes they'd like to see available close to home. Then build those offerings into your community or adult education program. Keep schools open long enough to accommodate these classes. It could pay dividends for the schools in both understanding and revenue.

Some businesses invite students into their operations for tours, internships, or special projects. Through these projects, students find out about different careers and job experiences, and businesses can promote future employment opportunities to potential candidates.

Many school administrators are suggesting policies to their school boards that will support establishing school/business partnerships. When fundraising or the need for in-kind services or donations of equipment are important to the schools, enlightened school administrators meet with key staff members to develop a "wish list" that they always carry just in case.

While contributions from business and industry can enhance a school program, schools should gain their primary support from taxpayers. Inequities in the size and wealth of businesses from one community to the next could lead to greater inequities among resources available to schools. Therefore, business support should supplement, not supplant, financial resources from the total community.

Schools and businesses are natural allies. Both are concerned about the short term and long term life of the community. A sound political alliance can help build support for better schools in the state legislature, in school bond and finance elections, and in other projects that lead to communitywide benefit.

The best way schools can serve the business community is by producing a quality product. Businesses require graduates who have the necessary skills to take their place in the working world or adults who have returned to school for retraining or an enhanced education. Ultimately, business people must understand that education is a sound investment in the future of their community, their state, and their nation.

Volunteers

Nonworking mothers once composed a great army of school volunteers. However, with an increasing number of mothers joining the work force, teachers can no longer depend on them to be there to bake cookies, cut patterns, or run a mimeograph machine. Those who are still available, though, are a goldmine for schools. As if a reduced volunteer pool weren't a big enough problem, some schools must contend with what can only be described as "volunteer burnout." But the economics of education and the need for community understanding and support make it necessary to maintain a pool of volunteers. The challenge is: How?

■ Understand burnout and avoid it. No one likes to think that what he or she is doing isn't important. And no one likes to perform the same routine task forever. Encourage teachers to plan work carefully so that volunteers can accomplish it. Vary the tasks and use their talents to the maximum within the time available.

Community Education Promotes Communication

The community education philosophy holds that education is for everyone, that education goes on at all times, and that education happens everywhere. Generally, a community education program in a school system has the benefit of a broadbased advisory committee and it often leads to in-depth surveys of the community's educational needs. Community education programs to meet those needs can lead to greater understanding between schools and the community, increased responsiveness, and improved public confidence in education.

In 1974, the U.S. Congress passed the Community Schools Act. The regulations for implementing that act listed eight minimum elements a program needed to be eligible for funds:

- **School involvement**—provides for the direct and substantial involvement of a public elementary or secondary school in the administration and operation of the program.

- **Community served**—serves an identified community, in most cases coextensive with the attendance area of the school.

- **Public facility as a community center**—concentrates services primarily in a specific public facility.

- **Scope of activities and services**—extends the activities and services offered by, and the uses made of, the public facility. For example, if a school is the community center, the concept encompasses the regular instructional program but also provides additional programs.

- **Community needs**—includes systematic and effective procedures for identifying, documenting, and responding to continuing needs, interests, and concerns of the community.

- **Community resources and interagency cooperative arrangements**—identifies and uses to the fullest extent possible the educational, cultural, recreational, and other existing and planned resources outside of the school; encourages and uses cooperative arrangements among public and private agencies to make maximum use of talents and resources and avoid duplication of services.

- **Program clients**—serves all age groups as well as groups with special needs not adequately served by existing programs in the community.

- **Community participation**—provides for the active and continuous involvement, on an advisory basis, of institutions, groups, and individuals in planning and carrying out the program, including assessments of needs and evaluations.

Excerpts from *Community Education: Managing for Success*, American Association of School Administrators, 1979.

- Broaden your horizons—look in new places for volunteers. Senior citizens, business people, high school students, and even working parents can be motivated to help if they are convinced their efforts will help students and if they can fit the assignment into their schedules.
- Develop a schedule of tasks and task assignments for each volunteer. Include the disclaimer, "Call me if this is inconvenient for you."
- Train both your staff and your volunteers. Teachers shouldn't take advantage of volunteers and give them all the "grunt work" to do. Volunteers shouldn't assume that because they are on campus, they now qualify as teachers.
- Follow up with volunteers. Ask their advice and impressions. It's that two-way communication again. Do some listening and you might find out what makes them happy and what distresses them—before they disappear.
- Don't forget to say thank you—two words that can't be said too often if they are said sincerely. Find new and creative ways to say thanks. If you don't have Happy Grams at your school, get some. Consider setting a day aside to honor volunteers. You could have a birthday club at your school, in which staff members take turns bringing treats for the people who help them so much. Certificates of appreciation also help.

Again, community education offerings can help answer the question, "What can we do for our volunteers?" Solicit their input on classes that the schools can offer. Consider giving volunteers discounts on community education fees as another way of saying thanks.

Working with Advisory Groups

If you think of advisory groups as cure-alls, as a means to divert criticism from the school system, as rubber stamps, you are well on your way to failure. An advisory committee is a council of people called together by schools to provide counsel on important issues, to perform tasks, to identify questions, to make suggestions, and to carry information about schools back into the community.

Advisory groups are effective for involving staff and community at both the local school and district levels. They can also address concerns, such as planning of playgrounds or reviewing the elementary math programs. Many superintendents have regular meetings of community-wide advisory councils.

Some communications departments meet a few times a year with communications advisory groups that might include: local public relations executives; reporters or managers from newspapers, radio or television; student editors; a journalism teacher; parents; an older citizen; and perhaps the superintendent and a board representative.

Because the PTA and other school-related groups may be uncomfortable with the formation of advisory groups, it's a good idea to have the PTA president, school principal, and advisory group chairperson appoint committee members on many of the committees. As a followup, the committee should report at the regular parent group meetings. This helps promote a feeling of trust and cooperation.

Like almost everything else, there is a right way and a wrong way to work with advisory groups. Here are some keys to success:
- Decide when you can use the input of an advisory group and when you can't. If it's a hard management decision that must be made, and you

know that the decision will be unpopular, you might ask for possible re-actions and how to deal with it. But don't run to the advisory group to simply try to take the heat off.

■ Define the group's task. That means telling them what is in their scope of responsibility and what is not. Be sure they understand they are advisory, not legislative.

■ Specify a timeline. The advisory group will convene on February 1 and complete its task by May 1, for instance. If the committee serves an on-going advisory role, stagger the membership terms so that the same people don't serve ad infinitum. Otherwise, you'll find yourself faced with an unofficial, unelected, unauthorized, mini-board of education.

■ Choose the membership carefully. Make sure it is representative and don't stack the membership in one direction or another. The public is too smart for that. Also, select members who will be conscientious and honorable. Let them know their participation is not intended as a platform so that they can run for political office.

■ Choose the chairperson carefully. You need a leader who is diplomatic, skilled in group dynamics, and not tainted with, as they say in political circles, "old baggage."

■ Provide a resource person from the school staff who can meet with the group regularly. This provides easy access to facts for the group and feedback to the district on the progress of the advisory group. It also lets the group know you feel its deliberations are important.

■ Let them know to whom they are reporting.

■ Don't give an advisory group busywork to do.

■ Act on the recommendations of any advisory group, whether in a positive or negative fashion. And tell the group why you're acting in that particular way. They invest time and talent in their task, and they deserve to know what you do with their recommendations.

■ Give the group the resources it needs to be successful. Whether that's coffee and doughnuts for meetings or secretarial support, make sure they have the resources to get the job done and feel good about it.

■ Don't doom them to failure by giving them an impossible task. Assign to advisory groups only those things that can be addressed by an advisory group. Let them know up front if you want reactions, suggestions, decisions, or completed tasks.

■ Thank them publicly and recognize their contributions when the job is done. That doesn't mean just a cursory thanks expressed verbally at a board meeting. Give group members a plaque or certificate acknowledging their accomplishments.

■ Don't just drop the group when the job is done. After serving on an advisory group, a person feels a vested interest in the schools. Your schools become their schools. Put them on the mailing list to keep them informed, or give them some other way to be involved.

A poorly conceived and poorly used advisory group can quickly turn into a pressure group. That's not the way to create positive experiences.

Working with Pressure Groups

What are pressure groups and what do they mean to schools? A pressure organization is part of the normal response process of people affected by ideas or decisions. Often these groups are responding to change or indicate that change is needed. These groups confront the school system when they feel their needs are not being met.

Although dealing with these groups can be difficult, pressure groups cannot be ignored by the schools. The greatest danger in dealing with these groups is to ignore them or aggravate a conflict to a point that communication is broken off. And, while the group's statements may only represent the opinions of a few leaders, these leaders are likely to remain vocal until the conflict is resolved.

Schools *can* deal effectively with pressure groups, especially if they follow some of these guidelines:

- Solicit input from the community on an ongoing basis. Listen and survey. If a group represents a significant portion of the community, it will probably have an effect on policies or programs. If it has little support or if its demands would be bad for education, you can point this out through various channels of communication. Knowing what the community is thinking in advance helps ensure that community needs are met and protects quality programs from destruction by a vocal few.
- Always try to work with an individual with a complaint. Ignoring them invites them to form a group. Deal with small groups, if possible.
- Look for a common denominator.
- Be adaptable, if adaptability is reasonable. Be willing to give a little on minor points so that you may stand firm on important points.
- Communication is key. The ultimate goal is to reach consensus through open discussion and fair negotiations.
- Clear the air. Eliminate myths or incorrect assumptions.
- Make an effort to understand a group's point of view and paraphrase it to avoid heated discussions. Show empathy.
- Be a good listener, and keep emotions in check.

Maintaining Cultural and Intellectual Integrity

A key to building healthy personal public relations is to know the communities we serve. A place to start in learning about a community is to study its demographics and review any opinion polls. However, true understanding of a community's culture goes beyond percentages in a study. What is the greatest source of community pride? What makes people laugh? What makes people cry? Who are the artists, the folk heroes, the preachers?

If you want to be a part of the community, then you must make an attempt to make the community a part of you. Learn as much as you can and proudly share with others what you've learned.

George Gallup once said that every school administrator should be an intellectual leader in the community. He urged school leaders to listen to their communities, to learn about educational needs, to generate discussion of those needs, and to build policies and programs that reflect them. "It's a natural instinct to build a bit of a fence around what we do," Gallup said, "but once you start with the conception that you are in charge of the intellectual development of the whole community, then you begin to think in larger terms. Almost instinctively, you bring more people into your world and inevitably do the right things."

You'll encounter some pressure groups with demands that will benefit education; others will press for changes that could hurt education. Regardless of the group and its demands, deal with the situation in a calm and open manner.

Working with Coalitions

People tend to band together when a common threat or opportunity arises. This is what coalitions are all about. A coalition is a group of organizations or individuals, often with diverse interests, formed to deal with a common issue or to achieve a common purpose.

A school district can help start coalitions. Bringing groups together to focus on issues increases understanding and support. Forming a coalition requires planning. Here are some of the steps in the process:

■ Explore the issues. The issue might be getting education back on the community agenda, or the issue might be more specific, such as extending the school year.

■ Identify groups—business leaders, nonparents, and/or others—that have a stake in the issue.

■ Convene a meeting. State the coalition's purpose as you see it.

■ Select a chairperson. The leader might or might not be someone directly involved in the issue. However, the chairperson might be someone with the time, energy, ability, and commitment to do the job.

■ Working together as a team, become informed and deal with the issue. Here are some guidelines for setting up successful coalitions:

■ Select members who will work not out of self-interest but out of concern for the common good.

■ Be sure members have the information they need to make wise decisions and encourage them to develop strategies to deal with the issues.

■ Be positive and look to the future.

■ Keep coalition members, your staff, board, and community informed through a communication network.

■ Avoid voting; work on the basis of consensus.

■ Don't insist that all groups deal with objectives in the same manner. Try to agree on general ideas and projects.

■ Be willing to make compromises for the common good. Be a good negotiator.

Coalitions dealing with issues concerning education are a natural part of the school and public relations program. By bringing together unique individuals and groups to work on a common concern, schools can turn diversity into unity that creates a consensus for education.

8

Working with

Government Officials

School administrators work hard to gain local board support for their budgets. They invest countless hours informing the community about a new program or tax need. Yet, not enough school officials are involved in an area of public relations that can reap major rewards for their school system. Working with government officials to ensure that education gets fair treatment is an important part of any public relations effort. Think about the last state action that made a difference in the quality of education in your schools. Consider a federal law or program that provided large chunks of money for needed programs. Think also about the regulation that prompted grief and wasted time and money and did little if anything to help students learn better. For these reasons alone administrators should be more attuned toward working in government relations.

Working with Government Officials

Some school districts have key administrators who handle legislative or governmental relations activities full time. Others do not. Either way, it is not possible to rest the total responsibility for this important function with one person or group of people or to delegate it entirely to representatives of professional associations or unions, even though these groups play a crucial role. All school employees play a part in helping or hindering government relations efforts.

More than Lobbying

The objective of a school system's governmental relations program might be: "To influence, mitigate, and/or lead the process for developing governmental policy and programs related to education."

When issues reach the decision-making stages in legislation, they often place the organization in a reactive role as they try to limit the damage done. That is why maintaining contacts with elected and appointed officials, conducting periodic surveys, and generally keeping an ear to the ground are so important. Identifying issues that could result in legislative action as they emerge gives the organization an opportunity to be in a proactive rather than reactive position. Instead of simply reacting to educational policy, the organization can play a key role in shaping it.

Government relations is more than lobbying for your school's position before the state legislature, governor, and/or congressional representatives. It involves a variety of other efforts, such as:

- Developing cooperative relationships with other organizations that share a common concern about legislative issues affecting education
- Providing leadership in dealing with various issues that have reached a government level of concern
- Working with regulatory agencies and various other members of the local, state, and federal bureaucracy
- Carrying on grassroots lobbying activities
- Stimulating the formation of coalitions to deal with issues that have reached a government level of concern
- Working with nonlegislative groups whose support might be needed to support or oppose legislation or regulations
- Responding to media inquiries on issues that are before legislative bodies
- Maintaining liaisons with the leadership of various political parties to determine their stands on educational issues, and on occasion, to help them shape their positions
- Keeping track of legislative trends in other states, regions, or communities
- Working with professional associations and unions to become part of a combined and stronger voice for good education policy.

A generic program may not always work. Therefore, a school system and its government relations administrator should select the approaches most appropriate for their objectives. The selection should be based on the uniqueness of the school district, the issue under consideration, and the potential reaction of those whose support is needed.

Lobbying

Three key words describe an effective lobbying and/or government relations effort: trust, confidence, and respect.

Some see lobbying as back-room politics, wining and dining, offering special favors, and vote buying. While it would be naive to dismiss the fact that some of these things go on, the primary purpose of lobbying is to provide elected and appointed decision makers with the information they need to make sound decisions. Lobbyists are most often respected individuals whose knowledge is sought and considered. Government officials may not always agree with your organization's position, but it is critical that they trust the lobbyist, believe the information provided, and realize that the lobbyist represents his or her constituency.

Effective representation requires avoiding or at least minimizing intuitive decision making on governmental issues. For example, don't say, "Let me tell you what I think our people would say." A more appropriate approach pays attention to acquiring knowledge of the subject, the process, and the people. Key steps in the process should be organizing and training volunteers and developing a communications network that provides data on issues essential to policy makers.

A proactive government relations program in a school system might include:

- Writing and initiating legislation, working through elected officials or various departments of government
- Negotiating with representatives of other groups, departments of government, and individual decision makers to reach consensus on an issue
- Conducting research to determine the potential effects of certain legislation or regulations
- Working closely with regulators because once a legislative decision is made, the process is far from over
- Providing expert information and analysis on issues government officials are considering.
- Preparing, coordinating, and providing testimony.

Members of the school administrative team, board of education, parent group representatives, and others can play key roles in the process.

Influencing members of Congress on positions they take on particular issues depends on understanding who and what influences them. The Columbia Institute for Political Research, in a survey devoted to determining what influences how a member of Congress votes on issues, reported that *local officials* and *other members of Congress are the two most important sources of information*. Add *constituent mail* and you have the three vital factors influencing the position a member will take on a particular issue.

Do Your Homework

Before you present an official position on an issue, do your homework. The time available to present the position is often short; to waste it on unsupported or unsupportable evidence would be a shame. Consider these suggestions:

- Analyze the issue. What is the potential impact on your school district and its programs? How can you measure the impact? What will it mean in terms of dollars, staffing, programs, and overall educational quality?
- Analyze the players. What other groups are likely to be affected? Who is the opposition? What are the likely positions, strengths and weaknesses? What do you know about the people behind the issue? What are their voting records on previous or similar issues? Who are our potential allies and coalition members? Why? What do you have to do to be successful? What do you potentially lose in fighting and winning?
- Know the process and the laws. You must know the decision-making process of the group with which you are working. What steps will the proposal go through? What happens if it is killed along the way?

Know the Law

Know the laws affecting your representation before legislators or decision makers. For example, in most states, a lobbyist must register and submit reports on expenditures used in influencing the government process. Some local governments have similar policies. In addition to doing it right, do it legally.

You Can't Do It Alone

One person can seldom do the job alone. He or she must often develop coalitions with other groups, individuals, school districts, and organizations. Some ad hoc coalitions are formed in response to threats to the institution. Some examples are the national Committee for Education Funding (concerned with budget cuts) and the National Coalition for Public Education (concerned with tuition tax credits). These types of coalitions have been effective in the political arena. Take time to evaluate the appropriateness of a coalition, though; coalitions can both advance and hinder an organization's efforts.

In addition, an effective government relations strategist will:

■ Issue news releases, encourage articles, explain positions to reporters or members of editorial boards.

■ Develop grassroots lobbying support, actively involving key communicators, parent and community groups, and others in writing personal letters and making phone calls explaining the position taken.

■ Seek the support of other government officials.

■ Find other organizations and experts on the issue who are willing to explain or even support the organization's position.

Ongoing Relationships

Working with government officials and the bodies or agencies they represent is not a one-shot deal. Effective communication between an organization and government is a daily process that goes beyond a special need to influence legislation or regulations. The difference between the amateur and the pro is that the amateur accepts the first "no" as the end of the process, while the pro sees it as the beginning. There is no finality in this type of process.

Most legislators or agency representatives will appreciate occasional invitations to visit the schools, to see first-hand how programs work, to see the effects of previous legislation or regulations, to become better informed and better able to serve their constituencies. Making it possible for those in government to experience what happens in schools is tantamount to professional development for many government officials. Most realize that a well-informed official stands a better chance of being re-elected or re-appointed.

Relationships are developed and maintained through regular contact. But not all that contact has to be official or take place only when we want something. Invite government representatives to attend school functions or just have lunch. Work to strengthen interpersonal communication. It helps when work must be more official.

Hints on Visiting Your Legislator

If you are scheduling a visit to one or some of your legislators, there are some guidelines to consider:

■ Send a letter first. The content of the letter should be organized into three parts: (1) introduction; (2) a summary section that includes what you want the reader to do, why it should be done, and any relevant data; and (3) a statement that includes both sides of the issue. Also, make it easy for the reader to respond.

- It often helps to ask an influential person to call and set the stage for your letter and personal visit.
- Common courtesy is a must—be prepared and on time; be brief and leave supporting materials to read (include a one- or two-page summary, if possible).
- Follow up with a thank-you letter.
- Stay in tune with events that might affect the issue or program. Doing so helps you become the immediate authority in handling follow-up questions and concerns.

Testimony Important

Occasionally, lobbyists will provide testimony. Often, lobbyists will make it possible for decision makers to hear directly from experts. A lobbyist brings together the experts and those needing the information.

Working with government officials at all levels requires that you represent a position to them and that you represent their position to your organization. Feedback is essential in developing the communication needed to work effectively in the legislative or decision-making arena with government officials.

9

News Media

Relations

The public schools of our nation are institutions in a democratic society, drawing their legitimacy from open, honest communication with their many publics. The news media represent one of the important channels for communication with the community, and schools should know how to work effectively with representatives of the print and broadcast media.

Much of what schools have to communicate is interesting information, but it doesn't necessarily qualify as news. That's why we need other channels for communication, in addition to the news media.

The best media coverage would probably be balanced, fair, accurate, and interesting. Good news coverage is not always good news. While we would much prefer to read about the successes of our schools, it is essential that our communities know about the problems we face.

Unless people understand the problems, it is sometimes difficult to justify the added resources to solve those problems and improve our schools. In addition, our publics know that no institution is perfect. Trying to pretend that schools are perfect by only sharing the good news with the media leads to major credibility problems with all of our publics, including news people.

Tips for Good Media Relations

You'll have a better working relationship with the media if you accept some basic facts. Reporters, editors, and publishers are not the monsters that many critics have made them out to be. They are men and women who are trying to do a good job. Just as one bad teacher does not mean all teachers are bad, one bad reporter or unbalanced news report doesn't mean all journalists are bad, either.

It is part of human nature to appreciate those who help us do our jobs. Administrators appreciate good teachers. Reporters appreciate cooperative, accurate, and available sources for their stories.

Even though you cooperate with a reporter over a period of time, or a newspaper covers your district's positive accomplishments, you are not exempt from coverage of negative news. The only way to reduce the possibility of negative news coverage is to avoid having negative things

67

happen or to do everything perfectly, usually impossible in any public institution.

Do not resent publishers, station managers or news reporters who cover the bad news about your school or district. Covering the news, both good and bad, is part of the journalist's job.

Here are some guidelines that can lead to a successful working relationship with the news media.

- Know your audience. Get to know the news editor or news director, the station manager, or the publisher. Learn who is responsible for covering education, sports, public service spots, and so on. Try to meet with these people personally, by having coffee or lunch, and ask how you can best meet their informational needs. Then use the advice they give you.
- Develop attractive news release and public service forms to carry information on a regular basis to your media list, public service list, sports list, and so on.
- Respond promptly to all inquiries from the news media, and make sure your staff also adheres to this policy. If a reporter calls and you are in a meeting, have the person answering the phone inquire about the reporter's deadline. If necessary and if possible, excuse yourself from the meeting and return the reporter's call. If the issue is controversial, your point of view may not be represented if you don't meet a deadline.
- If news media personnel can't make it to cover a story, offer to deliver some information to the newspaper or to provide a telephone report for radio stations.
- Know what is legally public information and what is not. Keep in mind that all reports and surveys are paid for by the public and are public property. You must provide this type of data to the news media if they request it.
- Remember that anything discussed during board meetings is part of board deliberations, and reporters can request to see the information as part of their coverage of a public body.
- Know what the "Sunshine laws" are in your state and adhere to them. Do not try to bend the rules to avoid media scrutiny. This practice will eventually backfire on you.
- Be aware of deadlines. Both weekly and daily newspapers have fixed deadlines. Old news is not news; so, missing deadlines is not in your best interest. Radio can take a story almost any time the newsroom is operating. Television is also becoming more of an instant medium, but for film and tape, time must be scheduled for shooting the story, processing, and editing.
- Avoid educational jargon, but if you have to use it, explain it.
- If you don't have the answer, don't try to make something up. Say, "I don't have that information right now, but if you'll give me a couple of minutes, I'll get it and call you right back."
- Understand that you can't always choose the time a reporter covers a particular story. You may want to release a story on Friday, but the reporter wants to do an advance on the event or the issue. Be as cooperative as possible under the circumstances. The reporter must answer to an editor or station manager.
- If your information includes complex numbers and figures, round them off accurately. And try to illustrate complicated financial issues with easy-to-understand charts, graphs, or comparisons.
- Use off-the-record statements judiciously—if at all. Should school ad-

ministrators ever tell a reporter things that they don't want to appear in the paper? Are there times when providing background information will help the reporter get the job done better? There is no clearcut answer, but if you do decide to go off the record, these suggestions might help: (1) Be sure you have a trust relationship with and respect for the reporter. Don't use "off-the-record" if you don't know the reporter well. (2) Realize that if the reporter gets the same information on the record from another source and uses it, that the trust has not been violated. (3) Be clear when you have gone off the record, and when you are again on the record. Don't jump back and forth.

■ Hold news conferences only when warranted. This usually means not very often. News conferences should be considered when: (1) the information you have to impart is of interest to many media people and should be released to everyone at the same time; (2) the information you have relates to a crisis and there is no time to individualize the story for all the different media; (3) the information you are releasing is of major importance and the media have been waiting for it; (4) the primary source of the information is available for only a limited time.

■ Never ask a reporter to show you a story before it is published.

■ Set up a good internal reporting system through which staff members can funnel news and feature story ideas to one person who has the responsibility for working with the media. A good backlog of story possibilities may be just what a reporter needs on a slow day.

■ Establish a communications advisory group, including news media representatives, to advise you on handling various problems involving communications. Use them as your feedback system to help evaluate your effectiveness in working with the media.

■ When giving a personal interview to a reporter, try to visit with the reporter first. Provide background information and get a feel for what information the reporter wants from you. This is especially useful when working with broadcast media.

■ Never say, "No comment." It will always look like a cover-up. Find a more constructive, polite way to explain why you cannot answer a given question.

■ If a reporter calls and you aren't the best source of the information he or she needs, don't transfer the call if there is any chance the call will be lost. Call back to let the reporter know who has the needed information, or get the information yourself and pass it along to the reporter. You might also initiate a call from the appropriate person to the reporter directly.

■ After you've made a statement or done an interview, let appropriate people in your organization know how you've addressed key issues. This approach avoids having several people from the same institution give conflicting information to the media.

■ If you expect the media to provide balanced, fair, accurate, and interesting coverage of your schools, make sure you are balanced, fair, accurate, and interesting in your dealings with them.

■ If a reporter has done what you consider a good job, don't forget to tell them so. Occasionally, let the reporter's boss know that he or she did a good job, as well.

Training for Your Staff and the Media

A wise superintendent or public relations director knows that the best way to raise the ire of media representatives is to try to slap a "gag order" on the rest of the staff. The districts that have tried to mandate that no one but the superintendent, public relations director, or other designated administrator may speak to the media have learned that lesson the hard way.

Not only does it arouse suspicion among reporters, the practice can cause morale problems among staff. This approach says to staff that you don't trust their judgment and that you are not keeping them well informed so that they can handle the questions.

You might involve media representatives in providing inservice training. A panel of reporters representing daily and weekly newspapers, and radio and television outlets can share tips for school people. After all, no one knows better than reporters what types of stories are used, and why, and what story ideas routinely find their way into "file 13."

Just as training is important for educators, it's also for the reporters who will regularly have the education beat. In some areas, education reporters have been on the beat for years and have an in-depth understanding of the issues. Too often, the education reporter is on the beat a short time and then moves on. The education writing profession needs the understanding and support of educators, just as educators need to be understood by the media.

Provide a thorough background briefing to any reporter newly assigned to your district. This briefing should include an overview of the district, a summary of major successes and of problems and issues facing the district, and local information on national issues such as testing, teacher competency, public confidence, and so on.

New reporters also appreciate a survival packet of helpful information. This can include publications such as the annual report, kindergarten or student handbook, personnel handbook, map of the district, internal telephone directory (whom to call for what), curriculum brochures, board brochure, and a table of organization. Share with the reporter your policy for dealing with the media in an open and honest manner.

How Do We Communicate Effectively with the Media?

There are several different ways to communicate with the news media, and the methods vary somewhat, depending on whether you are working with print or broadcast media.

News Releases

News releases call media attention to important information and events. However, don't expect that every story will be covered or that your release will make it into print as is. A news release generally calls attention to a story and reporters often follow up on it.

News releases should always be typed and doublespaced, leaving wide margins at the top and on both sides. This allows editors room to make editing and placement notes.

At the top of any news release, many professionals recommend that you type the date you issue the release, the date you are targeting it for

A Sample News Release

September 11, 19_____
For immediate release

STUDENTS AT JONES ELEMENTARY SCHOOL MAY APPEAR IN 'COURT'

This year students who don't take school rules and regulations seriously at Jones Elementary School will run the risk of being ticketed and summoned to "court."

Under a new system initiated by the staff of Jones Elementary, students who disobey playground or safety rules are issued tickets requiring them to appear in court. Two patrol members from each grade level issue tickets.

Once in court, a student may plead guilty or not guilty to a jury, composed of Student Council members. Council members will alternate as a judge. If the student pleads guilty, a penalty is levied. If the plea is not guilty, the judge and jury hear the student's, the patrol person's, and a witness's stories. The jury and judge meet to deliberate and make a decision on the case.

Penalties assigned are usually directly related to the type of rule the student broke. For example, a student found guilty of throwing papers may be assigned to pick up litter in the schoolyard.

According to Janet Smith, third grade teacher and project coordinator, "The court helps students learn to take responsibility for their actions, and they also learn the basics of our court system and how it works."

Anyone interested in observing the Jones Elementary Court process may attend the next session at 3:30 p.m. Tuesday, September 17, in the Jones Elementary School cafeteria.

For more information, contact: Elaine Johnson, Director of Communications
(777) 777-7777

Janet Smith, Jones Elementary teacher
(777) 777-7766

---

publication, your name as the contact person, and your office and possibly your home phone numbers. You won't get many calls at home, but considering the fact that media deadlines don't always correspond with your work hours, this information will be appreciated. If the release runs more than one page, type "more" at the bottom of each page. Type "30" or ### at the end of the release.

Use journalistic writing style. This means the most important information will be in the beginning of the story. Always address the major points: who, what, when, where, why, and how.

Use first and last names of all individuals mentioned in a story. Salutations such as Ms. Mrs. Mr., etc., may be used in school literature but are not consistent with today's journalistic style of writing. Make sure you send out your releases in a timely fashion. The story won't get any attention if it is about an upcoming event and it gets to the editor one day after the event has taken place.

Don't expect to see your stories appear in print the way you wrote them. They will be edited, rewritten, and shortened to fit space requirements. They may be ignored. Rarely do releases appear word for word. In some communities, though, local papers might depend on the schools to write stories and may even provide deadline dates for the releases and other information.

Fact Sheets

A fact sheet is a good way to get information to print and broadcast media. It gives all the main facts, the answers to the who, what, when, where, why, and how questions. It provides a contact person whom the reporter can get in touch for more information. It allows reporters to develop stories in their own styles.

The fact sheet approach is effective for educators who are not accustomed to writing in journalistic style. The fact sheet allows you to organize your thoughts, share all the appropriate information, and let the reporters do what reporters do best. Some small weekly newspapers prefer news releases because they don't have the staff to rewrite a fact sheet.

Backgrounders

Different from a news release or a fact sheet, a backgrounder explains the background of a story idea or situation. Backgrounders are often attached to fact sheets as a way to give more information to reporters or editors.

The term "backgrounder" also refers to a face-to-face meeting between an information source (the superintendent or public relations director, for instance) and one or more reporters. The purpose of the meeting is not to solicit any particular story but to give background information on an issue, event, or the school system itself.

News Conferences

As mentioned earlier, news conferences should be scheduled rarely and only when the information or event warrants. They take a lot of time and reporters are not particularly fond of them, especially if there is no news.

If you do call a news conference, make sure you have something significant to share. Schedule the conference at a time and location convenient for the majority of reporters.

You may want to schedule a news conference at a location that illustrates the information you are releasing. A news conference to announce a new reading program might be held in a reading resource room where students are actually using the program. That way the media can get the photos or videotape they need for a good story.

The public relations director, if you have one, will usually coordinate a news conference. This means getting to know the reporters who are there, locating electric outlets for the broadcast media (if they need them), making sure that AV equipment is adequate and in working order, preparing and providing press kits for those who attend, and opening and closing the conference. When several electronic media are present, you may want to provide a "multbox" that allows several people to plug into your sound system.

You have time at the beginning of a conference to present your information and any remarks by "experts" who could enhance the story. Do not prolong a news conference. Allow enough time but don't overdo it. Sometimes, you could schedule a press availability rather than a press conference. At an availability, the news source doesn't necessarily make a statement but is available for questions. Coffee, juice, and doughnuts or rolls are often appreciated at news conferences.

Public Service Announcements

One of the most common public relations uses of radio and television is the public service announcement (PSA). Despite changing regulations, most radio stations still provide free time, especially for good local spots. Serving the local schools helps to build audiences. Talk with station managers and program directors. Find out what their policies are and the best way to produce PSAs, either in-house or at the station.

Some tips for doing a PSA:

- Develop public service announcement form that includes the name, address, and phone number of your school system and the name of a contact person. If you do not have this form, be sure the information is visible on the page.
- Place the current date on the form.
- Indicate the length of the spot, and if you are preparing more than one PSA, give each a number, such as: 1-30, 2-30, 1-60, and so on.

Public Service

Anywhere Community Schools, District 00, 909 Anywhere Street, Anywhere, California, 500-678-9876

30-Second Public Service Announcements
Summer School
TO AIR UPON RECEIPT THROUGH MAY 30

1-30 Elementary
Now's the time to enroll your children in the District 00 Elementary Summer School Program. An exciting array of courses is being offered, ranging from developmental math and reading ... to music, ecology ... and even television production. For further information, or to enroll, call 678-1234 now. That's 678-1234 to enroll in the District 00 Elementary Summer School.

2-30 Junior and Senior High
Junior and Senior High students! Don't wait a minute longer. Enroll now in the District 00 Summer School. Some of the interesting and exciting courses being offered include: driver education, motorcycle safety, art, English, math ... and an array of music, social studies, and science courses. Call the District 00 Summer School office at Westside High, 678-3987, now to enroll.

- Include a line indicating what the spot is about, such as "Kindergarten Roundup."
- Indicate when the spot should begin and the last air date. For example, "To air upon receipt through August 14."
- If an event takes place over an extended period of time, you may want to produce two sets of spots, one to run prior to the event and one to run during the time the event is taking place.
- Copy should be written in fairly short sentences, as you would speak. Long sentences on radio are unnatural and often fail to communicate.
- Bring the spot to life with interesting copy, and if appropriate, use cuttings from interviews, background music, or sound effects. Music and sound effects are usually available in the radio station music and production libraries or at commercial recording studios. Some school systems have their own recording facilities.
- Read your announcements aloud to ensure that they capture and maintain attention, they can be read easily, and contain pertinent facts, such as who, what, when, where, why, and how. Make sure the spots fulfill your purpose for them.
- Consider adding actual sound to your spots. Using a good quality tape recorder, record a student reading an original essay, giving a speech, or orally working through a math problem. Add your own copy before and after the actuality and you'll bring more life to your spot.
- Be sure your PSAs are the right length; time them. Most spots preferred by radio stations will run 10 or 30 seconds. Some stations will air 60-second spots.
- Check with your local radio stations to see if they will accept pretaped PSA's. Some will use only straight copy that someone there reads on the air.

Television stations use public service announcements, too, but they are visually designed and cost more to produce. Check with your local television stations. Sometimes they are willing to work with you to produce PSAs at no cost if they believe that the spots are in the public interest.

Telephone Calls

The most effective way by far to get your message to the news media is a personal phone call. It is to the print media, you can give the reporter some information on the story you have in mind and ask if he or she would like additional information in writing.

If you're calling a television assignment editor, summarize your story idea in as few words as possible, emphasizing the visual aspects of what you have in mind. If it's radio, your remarks might be recorded on the air, so be prepared.

It is acceptable to call the media and alert them about stories or upcoming events. However, don't make a pest of yourself. It's okay to make a follow-up call to make sure that material was received and ask if there are any questions. Don't oversell and don't get upset if the reporter chooses not to cover the story.

Tip Sheets

Tip sheets provide reporters with a variety of story ideas on a regular basis. Instead of doing one news release or one fact sheet, summarize several story ideas in one or two paragraphs each, type it, and provide the name of a contact person to reach for further information.

This way, reporters and editors choose the stories that most interest them. You will be appreciated for keeping them supplied with good ideas.

One caution: Make sure the ideas you provide are, indeed, good ones and not just puff pieces that can't be developed into news or feature stories.

NOTEA PUBLIC SCHOOLS

TIP SHEET

Your name _____

Work phone _____ Home phone _____

School/Department _____

Date _____

There's a News Story Here ....

☐ for external publication*
☐ for the Note-A-Genda (check one or both)

Who:

What:

When:

Where:

Why:

How:

Photo Suggestion:

Fold, staple and mail to the Community Relations Office Through Interschool Mail.

*Request newspaper or TV coverage one to two weeks in advance.
**For Note-A-Genda, story ideas must be received by the Friday before publication.

Interviews

Many interviews are live. You can't edit what you're going to communicate, as you can when you write. Once you've said something, you can't take it back. That's why preparing for interviews and understanding how to handle them is so important.

If you know you're going to have an interview for radio or television, for instance, brainstorm with a colleague the potential tough questions you might be asked. Formulate possible responses in advance.

When working with the broadcast media, make sure you keep your responses brief and language alive and descriptive. It will increase the chance of having quotes used. Brevity is a good rule when working with any media people; it makes you more quotable and lessens the opportunities for mistakes that result in misquotes. The broadcast media look for brief sound bites that carry important information clearly, accurately, and colorfully.

When doing an interview for television, remember that nonverbal communication is as important as what you say. You posture, your facial expressions, the position of your arms and the use of your hands all communicate along with your words.

Talk Shows

Radio talk shows can be a very effective channel for communication if you take the time to prepare properly. Preparation for a talk show consists mainly of understanding the nature of the medium and rehearsing for some of the tough questions you might encounter. Here are some tips on how to handle typical situations that arise during a program of this type:

- Be cordial to listeners at all times. However, be firm when needed.
- Be a good listener. Try to listen for the point the caller is trying to make.
- Be candid with the caller.
- Be interesting and lively.
- Politely explain what the facts really are when you encounter misinformation or misunderstanding from callers.
- Always express gratitude to the people who have called to comment or ask questions and to the station for making the opportunity possible.
- Let people know you are interested in their ideas, opinions, and questions.
- If a caller wishes to discuss a school employee, ask that the person call the appropriate office at a suggested time in lieu of discussing the individual on the air.

Board Reports

Many radio stations appreciate a brief report following board meetings. Check with your local news directors in advance to determine their interest and the steps they'd like for you to follow.

Generally, it's important to write a brief summary of the major action taken at the meeting. Try to summarize what you have to say in 30 to 60 seconds and practice reading what you've written prior to calling the radio stations. As you do the report, be conversational and be prepared for questions.

If you've worked it out in advance with the news department, the announcer on duty will be receptive when you call. If not, just explain what the arrangements are and ask if the announcer would like to accept a brief school board meeting report from you. If they are short-staffed, television stations and newspapers often appreciate hearing about highlights of the meeting for possible followup. A cardinal rule: Always be honest and don't avoid reporting controversy. Otherwise your credibility will suffer, and future reports will not be used.

Cable Television

Cable television is an often overlooked electronic media available to help school people tell their story and used frequently in instruction. Now it can also be used as a public relations tool.

Besides using cable television to provide live broadcasts of board meetings, some districts are also using cable as an instructional tool for students, who staff the cameras and produce the program.

While some school boards worry about potential grandstanding by individual members if the meetings are broadcast live, most veterans of this practice indicate that this is not normally a problem. There are some cautions to keep in mind if you move to live broadcasts of your board meetings, however.

Do a practice run-through of how the system works going on the air. Give board members and key administrators training in what to wear, how to apply make-up, nonverbal communication, how to work with the microphone, and to avoid things that might embarrass them.

Videotape a session and play it back for the participants with a trained discussion leader who can help critique the performance. Cable television is also an excellent medium for special interest shows related to the schools. However, programs need to be promoted to boost the audience share.

Some local communities are even presenting their own local news programs. One community in Arizona, served by the Cox Newspaper chain headquartered in Atlanta, started a "newspaper channel." The station features a preview of the next day's news stories, with lots of community service programming and special features shows sprinkled throughout the day. It's a natural for getting the school message to the local public.

Guest Editorials/Weekly Columns

Another technique that is used around the country, in both newspapers and on radio or television, is the guest editorial or weekly column. The editorials are usually presented by the superintendent, a board member, administrator, or sometimes teachers.

When done for radio, editorials might run 60 to 120 seconds. If you use this technique, remember the rules for writing for radio as opposed to writing for print. Keep your words and your sentences short. Minimize the use of jargon. Make it warm and conversational. Try to draw word pictures to help your audiences see what they're hearing.

The guest column or editorial in the newspaper is usually featured on a weekly basis, with comments solicited from the board or superintendent. These are often written with the assistance of the public relations executive. Op-ed pieces are also useful. These columns normally appear opposite the editorial page.

The columns should focus on issues of local concern, problems as well as successes, and local angles to national education stories. If done well, they can be a big boost to your overall communications program.

Posting Menus

If you air the daily menu on radio each morning, couple the information with news or facts about education. This information can include announcements, tips on how parents can help their children at home, information on new programs in the schools, construction updates, board meeting agendas, and so on.

Community Service Programming

What do you do if you're asked to be a guest on a radio or television community service program that you know is only aired at odd hours? Accept graciously and remember that the show wouldn't be on the air if it didn't have an audience.

Prepare for these programs just as you would for an interview or any other radio or television appearance. Since they're usually taped in advance, try to have a plan to help increase the number of people who tune in to the program. You may be able to help the station build the audience for the program, thus securing a better time slot for it in the future.

Radio and Television Programs

In many communities, local radio and television stations offer the schools an opportunity to do regular programs. Occasionally, school systems turn down the opportunity since officials may not feel the time slot for the program will attract a large enough audience. However, effective public relations involves continuous communication. While the program may only reach a few thousand viewers or listeners this week, it may eventually touch the lives of thousands of listeners or viewers.

When doing a school system program on radio or television, make the program lively. Include some heated discussion on what people want to know about. If you are doing a half-hour television program, consider breaking it up into segments to keep the viewer interested. For example, the program might begin with an upbeat number from a school music group, followed by a ten-minute interview on school enrollment declines, another number from the student music group, a teacher and students demonstrating a compelling science experiment, an interview with the superintendent, and a final number from the music group, which plays as the program signs off.

If you receive an offer to do a program, do it if at all possible, and make it interesting. If you have not received an offer to do this type of program and would like to pursue the idea, talk to program directors at local radio and television stations or cable systems.

Crisis Communications

Crisis communications is one of the most difficult aspects of media relations, but it, too, can be handled efficiently and effectively. The key is to have a crisis communications plan and to understand media needs when dealing with a breaking news story.

Crisis communications usually means bad news, although the bad news may not be something that impacts your school or district negatively. You may simply be an incidental participant in a much larger story.

Some examples of crisis communication that require a representative of the school district to get involved:

- On a snowy day, a school bus is struck by a gravel truck, sending several students to the hospital for treatment
- A bomb threat is received by one of the schools
- A student is injured on the way to or from school or while off campus during the lunch hour
- One of your schools is torched by an arsonist in the early morning hours
- Teachers union announces strike beginning at midnight.

These crises all have one thing in common—all will attract the attention of health or law enforcement agencies and probably the local news media. Any situation reported to the fire department or local police authorities earns the media's attention since all newsrooms are equipped with police scanner radios. If the fire department or police are called in to deal with a situation, assume that the media know it.

You will be able to deal more effectively with the media during a crisis if your district has developed a crisis communications plan. Your plan should be based on reporting fact, not rumor. While plans vary from district to district, each should address the following questions:

- Who is responsible for coordinating communication in a crisis?
- What constitutes a crisis?
- How is information fed to the communications coordinator in a crisis?
- How will information be released in a crisis and who should receive it?
- What rights of privacy prevail, and what constitutes the public's right to know?
- What follow-up procedures must be followed?
- What law enforcement agencies might be involved, and what kind of coordination must there be with the responsible parties in these agencies and their communications teams?
- Is the communications director authorized to release factual information?
- What are the procedures if the superintendent is out of town or unavailable for some other reason?
- How is the crisis communications plan communicated to all other members of the management team and the board?

School officials will find that it is sometimes to their advantage to initiate contact with media during a crisis situation, rather than waiting for the media to call and then responding from a defensive posture. If you know a situation will attract the attention of the media, get your facts together, anticipate the questions the media will ask, and get those answers. Then, pick up the phone and release the information yourself.

By doing this, the media will be more understanding when you tell them there is some information, because of privacy laws, that you can't disclose. They'll appreciate the effort you made on their behalf.

10

Publications

Publications are among the most effective channels of communication for conveying information about the schools to various internal and external publics. School publications should reflect the careful planning necessary to ensure that a publication's objectives are met in its content and design. To do so, a publication must address any key questions and be responsive to the needs and interests of its readers.

When possible, try to use professionals whose job it is to write and design publications. Under most circumstances, you will find that your publications and products are more effective. For those times that you must produce publications without professional assistance, we offer some basic guidelines to follow.

Planning

You wouldn't adopt a new reading program without going through an extensive planning process. Your publications also deserve adequate planning.

To begin, *define your purpose*. Why are you going to produce this publication? What objectives do you hope to accomplish by using this particular channel of communication? Are you publishing to inform or to motivate? Do you have some action you want the reader to take after reading the publication? What kind of impression do you want the publication to create?

Next, *define your audience*. A publication, written and designed one way, won't necessarily communicate effectively with all your internal and external audiences. Understand also what your audience knows about the topic. Know their comfortable reading level, how busy they are, and appreciate the challenge you have in getting them to read what you've written. For example, busy teachers stopping at their mailboxes may not be interested in a three-page memo. They might respond more readily to three well-written paragraphs. In addition, relate what you write to your readers' experiences and interests and avoid jargon.

The various audiences you must consider are: taxpayers, senior citizens, educators, support staff members, students, substitute teachers, and so on.

Prior to putting anything on paper, decide which audiences you want to reach. Make sure the publication's purpose correlates with the audiences for the final product.

When you have determined purpose and audience, you can *determine the format*. Of course, many of your decisions on the format you choose are also based on your budget for the publication. Will it be black ink on white paper, or do you have the budget to add color? Do you have to go with a standard 8½ × 11-inch sheet, or can you afford an off-sized publication? Will it be a tabloid on newsprint, a brochure on glossy or coated stock, or will you stick with a standard matte finish?

The answers to these questions come from two areas of consideration—your publication's purpose/audience and your budget. The advantage of having professionals employed by the district or from the outside work on your publications is that they know how to get the most mileage from your budget to serve your purposes.

Professionals, however, do follow certain guidelines based on readability and positive reader response. For instance, if you're doing a newsletter or other publication that contains a lot of copy, use black, dark brown, or dark blue ink on white, buff, or pale yellow paper. Anything else could be difficult to read. Bright ink colors such as red are not usually good except to accent or provide interest.

According to research in the newspaper advertising business, adding a second color to an ad increases the response rate by 60 percent. If you have the budget, you might want to add color to the design of a publication like the school calendar.

Most professionals explore all sizes and shapes in deciding format, quite often resorting to some application of the 8½ × 11-inch format—two-fold business envelope size, 5½ × 8½ inches, or the standard full size. Keeping your design to a standard size paper keeps paper costs down and makes the piece easier to mail.

When choosing a paper stock, go back to your purpose. If you're using photos, consider how your paper choice will affect the photos. As a rule of thumb, don't print photos on colored paper or with colored ink. People with blue, red, or green faces are not appealing. In other words, if the photos are an important element of your publication, be careful to present them well.

With any paper, you need to consider opacity; in other words, is the paper heavy enough so that what's printed on one side of the paper doesn't show through on the other side?

Content

You've done your initial planning. You know what you want to accomplish, who the publication is for, and the format you're going to use. It's now time to determine the content of your publication.

Don't assume that you know everything that should go into a publication or that the administrator in charge of the department producing the publication has all the answers either, although that person will surely be a primary source.

If your project is a kindergarten handbook, work with an advisory committee of kindergarten teachers and parents of four- and five-year-olds. The teachers will tell you what they think should be in the handbook, and the parents will tell you what they need and want to know.

If it's a substitute teacher handbook you're preparing, get some guidelines from the personnel director. Spend time with both veteran and novice substitute teachers, and talk with regular teachers. That way your publication will really fulfill its purpose and meet the needs of your audience.

One of the most commonly produced school publications is the school or district newsletter. Some guidelines for the content of newsletters might include stories that address:

- News of what's being taught, why it's being taught and how
- School board decisions that affect your school or district and opportunities for parent and community involvement.
- Achievements of students, teachers, administrators, and support staff
- A calendar of events (holidays, special events, student activities, school board meetings)
- Testing: when, why, how, and what it all means to students
- Interesting facts, such as a "Did you know?" column
- Problems, as well as successes, with information on how you are working to solve the problem and how others may help
- Reports on advisory group deliberations
- Invitations to visit or volunteer
- Requests for reader comments or queries and a section for presenting them
- Local angles to national education stories.

Samples of Award-Winning School District Publications

The content of every newsletter should include the logo or name of the newsletter at the top of the first page and a section of each issue where you tell people: the name of the newsletter, name of the school or district, address, telephone number, editor's name, names of other staff members, and whom to call for more information.

Remember, the content of a publication must support the purpose you have established for the publication, and it must address the communication needs of the audience you're trying to reach.

Writing

When you're writing a publication to represent your school or district, you're not writing for a university dissertation panel. Big words, long sentences, and jargon have no place in the world of educational publications for the general public. They serve only as barriers to understanding.

When you write and design a publication, remember the 30-3-30 rule. Most readers fall into one of three categories; they'll read your publication for 30 seconds, three minutes, or 30 minutes.

Some editors expect readers to spend 30 minutes on a story. While this might be desirable, it isn't realistic. The truth is, most readers fall into the 30-second or three-minute categories. Your writing, as well as the way you organize items on a page, should respect the reader's time.

Try to write using the news style of professional journalists. Answer the questions of who, what, when, where, why, and how in your writing, and put the most important information at the beginning of each of your stories.

Newspaper editors recommend that sentences should average about 17 words in length. Be careful, too, not to use too many words of three syllables or more. They make reading more difficult, and readers feel they have to wade through your publication. Donald Hymes, director of publications of the Montgomery (Maryland) County School District, provides excellent guidelines on how to write to be understood in his "20 Rules for Good Writing." His rules are:

1. Prefer the plain word to the fancy.
2. Prefer the familiar word to the unfamiliar.
3. Prefer the Saxon word to the Romance.
4. Prefer nouns and verbs to adjectives and adverbs.
5. Prefer picture nouns and action verbs.
6. Never use a long word when a short one will do.
7. Master the simple declarative sentence.
8. Prefer the simple sentence to the complicated.
9. Vary your sentence length.
10. Put the words you want to emphasize at the beginning or end of your sentence.
11. Use the active voice.
12. Put statements in a positive form.
13. Use short paragraphs.
14. Cut needless words, sentences, and paragraphs.
15. Use plain, conversational language. Write the way you talk.
16. Avoid imitation. Write in your natural style.
17. Write clearly.
18. Avoid gobbledygook and jargon.
19. Write to be understood, not to impress.

20. Revise and rewrite. It can always be improved.

Another good way to evaluate your writing is to test it for reading level. The average American reads at a ninth grade level; many read below that. We also know that most readers are more comfortable reading one or two levels below their maximum.

Many writers use the *Gunning Fog Index*™ to help them evaluate the reading level of their writing. To determine the fog index of your writing, take a 100-word sample of something you've written and apply these steps:

- Find the average number of words per sentence in the sample. (If the final sentence in the sample runs beyond the 100th word, use more than 100 words to compute the average for this step.)
- Count the number of words in the 100-word sample containing three syllables or more. (Do not count proper nouns or three-syllable verb forms ending in -ed or -es.)
- Add the average number of words per sentence to the number of words containing three or more syllables and multiply the sum by 0.4.

For example: A 100-word passage contains an average of 20 words per sentence and 10 words of three or more syllables, the sum of these two factors is 30 (20 plus 10). Multiplying 30 by 0.4 gives a fog index of 12.

The results of these calculations is a "reading level" with these equivalents:

Fog Index	By Grade
17	College graduate
16	College senior
15	College junior
14	College sophomore
13	College freshman
12	High school senior
11	High school junior

A good guideline to remember when writing so that you'll be understood is to write conversationally and warmly. Above all, use proper grammar, spelling, and punctuation when writing something that is going to represent an educational institution.

Layout and Graphics

Your writing can be perfect, clean and informative, but if you don't place the words on the page correctly, you still may not get your message across.

Start with an understanding that you do not have to fill every single space on the page with your message. Leave a little "white space," or places where there is no type or graphic element. This will help give the reader's eye a rest and put the focus on the information that is important.

When a page is full of type and has no breaks, it looks gray and unappealing. Readers subconsciously brace themselves for the tedious job ahead and look for any excuse not to read. You can encourage readers by presenting the copy in such a way that they are drawn to the page. White space on the page is not the only available art element that makes a page appealing. Photographs and clip art—mass-produced illustrations you can buy commercially—are other inexpensive but effective resources.

You can also create visual breaks in the text itself by using these various methods:

- *Subheads* provide readers with an outline of the major topics, are separated from the text and highlighted with bolder, bigger type than the text type.
- *Bullets,* such as small round dots or squares, emphasize the elements of a list that has been pulled out from a paragraph. Rather than list items in paragraph form, list them with bullets, as we did here.
- *Indent* all paragraphs and all lists. If a list is a sublist, double your indentation.
- *Boxes,* with or without screens—highlight important points, case stories, or issues by setting the information off in a ruled box. To emphasize and create more of an art element, screen (shade) the area.
- *Color,* if used effectively, highlights and provides art interest.
- Extra space can be used to separate and introduce lists or new sections.

Typography is another important graphic element. That's why it's important to choose the right type for your purpose. When you have material that requires a lot of reading, most publications professionals recommend that you use what is called serif type. Serif types have extra lines or curlicues added to the upper and lower strokes of a letter. If the extra lines are not too decorative, they enable readers' eyes to move easily so that they perceive words and phrases instead of individual letters. The other kind of typeface is sans serif (without serif). Sans serif typefaces, because they are clean and straight looking, are used more often than serif for headlines or charts.

This is serif. This is sans serif.

The unwritten rule for good readability is to use a clean serif typeface for any text that requires a lot of reading. Most sans serif typefaces and some elaborate serif types are too hard on readers' eyes. Choice of type for headlines is now considered flexible, according to your design. Some people like a big change; so, they use a sans serif typeface for headlines; others change by using a different serif type. The most important rule regarding headlines and readability is that upper and lower case letters in headlines are more readable than all capital letters.

Also when you are writing headlines, remember to include a verb to make them more interesting. Headlines should grab readers and draw them in. For example, "Fourth Grade News" serves as a nice label, but "Fourth Graders Plant Trees as Part of Study" encourages reader involvement.

If you have the budget, professionally typeset copy is usually preferable to typewriter type. However, typewriter type does add a sense of immediacy; so, remember your purpose before you spend the money. If you are using typewriter type, you could have headlines set commercially for a more professional look. Other less expensive methods of getting professional-looking headlines are to use the press-on letters available in most office supply stores or to try some of the headliner machines on the market.

The size of type you use is important for readability also. The recommended size for body copy is 10-point. Using anything smaller jeopardizes readability. For subheads, 14-point is usually a good choice, while 24- or 30-point works well for headlines. (Point refers to a measurement term in professional typesetting.) Of course, all of theese are recommended sizes that will vary according to your purpose and needs. It's a good idea, too, to allow extra space above subheads. It cues the reader subtly that a change is taking place and shows off the head more.

Be careful not to set your columns too wide or too narrow. If you're working with an $8\frac{1}{2} \times 11$-inch sheet, you would want a two-column or three-column format. A rule of thumb for column widths is to never exceed twice the alphabet. In other words, a column should not exceed 52 characters. On the other hand, you need to avoid such narrow columns that every line has a hyphenated word at the end.

Use of Photography

It's been said that one picture is worth 1,000 words. If that's so, a good photograph helps you reach those 30-second and three-minute readers, *but only if it's good.*

The "stand-em-up-and-shoot-em" school of photography should be used as a last resort. The same goes for check-passing, handshaking, and award-giving pictures. These kinds of photographs, while sometimes necessary for political reasons, have little or no positive impact on readers.

The best photographs show action or emotion, include one to four people, and illustrate an event, activity, or concept. If possible, the shot should be a closeup so that the participants are easily recognizable.

Black and white photographs work best for what most school districts can afford in printing costs. All the photos should be good quality, black-and-white photographs. Instant camera reproductions and color snapshots printed with black ink often become soft on focus and muddy.

Distribution

How are you going to get your publication to your readers? Will you mail it? Will you hand it out at parent teacher conferences? Is it going to be distributed at kindergarten registration?

Distribution of a publication must be discussed in the planning phase, because it has an impact on budgets, timelines, and formats. It also impacts your layout, since some publications are "self-mailers" with pre-printed postage stamps and space set aside for address labels. Others are designed to be mailed in special envelopes or distributed person-to-person. In determining your distribution system, try to get the most for your money while at the same time not losing sight of purpose and audience.

A general interest newsletter representing a school district and issued on a monthly or quarterly basis should perhaps be sent to parents and other important publics such as nonparent taxpayers and local business people. If financially possible, a quarterly newsletter or publication should be sent to all the households in your area. To save on the costs, and if time is not of the essence, consider third class bulk mail for the distribution.

When using bulk mail, check with your local postmaster before designing and printing your publication, and explore the possibilities of mailing to "postal customer local." This option is available to schools, but many educators, as well as postal officials, are not familiar with this low-cost approach to reaching all households within a particular postal distribution route.

Evaluation

Evaluation of publications is as important as the evaluation of any other aspect of a communications program.

Your evaluation methods will vary depending on the type of publication you have produced. Newsletters can be evaluated through informal feedback on an ongoing basis. Use an annual reader survey, written or telephoned, for more formal feedback.

A questionnaire targeted to a representative sample of your reader audience can effectively evaluate handbooks and brochures. The kindergarten handbook can be evaluated by surveying kindergarten teachers and parents of kindergarteners. The staff handbook can be evaluated by asking the staff how effective it is, and so on.

Professional evaluations are also available for a fee, both on a local and national basis. And publications contests, with evaluations included at a modest increase in the entry fee, can also be helpful.

Most publications in educational communications can be divided into two categories: those designed for internal publics and those geared toward external publics. Here are some examples of both:

Internal publications

- Staff newsletter—produced regularly and distributed to all staff members, not just those with teaching certificates.
- Board reports—brief summaries of board meetings distributed to staff (and sometimes other key people in the community) the morning after a board meeting. These must be written in an objective style, never leaving out controversial issues or simply providing a showcase for the board, or they will not be considered credible communications vehicles.
- Substitute teacher handbooks—written and designed to make substitute teachers feel more welcome and be more effective.
- Staff handbooks—consider doing a version for certified staff and one for support staff (be careful to make sure they are equal in quality). Look for ways to develop a staff handbook that will be used rather than filed in the bottom drawer. A calendar format is one way to produce a "keeper."
- Curriculum guides—while these include a lot of technical educational information, care should also be given to clarity of writing and an attractive layout and design. Think about ease of use.

- Paycheck stuffer—used on an "as needed" basis, this is a good vehicle for bringing employees' attention to important information or upcoming events.

External publications

- Student handbook—write and design this so that it will be read and used by the students. Avoid legalistic language. Remember, students are often sophisticated in their exposure to visual media.
- Community newsletter—a popular publication at the district level and often at the building level. In a district where many households do not have children in school, newsletters can be very effective. Do the newsletter well. Remember, you have a lot of competition for your reader's time.
- Parent newsletter—often produced at the school level and distributed primarily to parents. Consider providing training for those responsible for parent newsletter production. Expand your distribution system by dropping off extra copies at doctor's offices and beauty and barber shops within the school's attendance area.
- Program brochures—these could focus on kindergarten, special education offerings, Chapter I, gifted, or other special programs. These are designed for a specific audience and are not always of interest to everyone.
- Finance report—can be published as a discussion guide before adopting the annual budget or produced after the budget is set to explain how taxpayer's money is being used to benefit students.
- Annual report—an overview of the school district, explaining pertinent facts and figures, objectives for the coming year, and the accomplishments of the previous year.
- Facts and figures—often called a "fingertip facts" publication because it provides a thumbnail sketch of your district in a brief format.
- Election voter guides—if your local ordinances allow, you can publish a guide to explain an upcoming budget or finance election. This sort of publication, when allowed, cannot advocate a "yes" or "no" at taxpayer expense.

11

Using Technology in Public Relations

Some school districts have already advanced far into the technology age; others are still in the beginning stages. Those that have already begun have discovered what the rest will find out—microcomputers, word-processors, cable television—all provide a wealth of opportunities to improve a school district's public relations program. The equipment can be used to:

- Save time and money preparing publications, contracts, and other documents
- Speed up handling of correspondence
- Provide up-to-date education news and other timely information to staff members
- Personalize and speed up the processing of news releases and mailing lists
- Process survey data and develop personalized campaign efforts for adult/community education classes or to finance educations
- Involve the members of the community more in school projects and increase their awareness of what the students are doing
- Connect schools and members of an administrative team electronically through a computer network
- Track issues.

These are only some of the practical administrative uses of technology. As more administrators acquaint themselves with the capabilities of modern technology, they'll find more ways to make the education process more effective.

Preparing Publications

School districts prepare a variety of publications: newsletters, brochures about special programs, staff directories, annual reports, school calendars, and contracts and others. Copy for these publications must be written and typed. Then, in many cases they have to be typeset, pasted up, and printed commercially or in-house. These procedures all involve several people and require certain steps that can make it difficult to produce timely publications.

With the advent of microcomputers (or word processors) publications operations for school districts have been revolutionized. For example, publication of a school district's staff directory, a complex process, could require dozens of hours of combined labor for document preparation, composition, and proofreading. But, using the convenience of microcomputers with word processing, a school district could reduce the time, labor, and costs by as much as 70 percent.

A school district that spends an average of $5,000 for typesetting its publications each year could possibly reduce these external costs or free funds for other publications. With microcomputers and good software, people in-house can write, edit, and proofread original drafts, code in a typesetter's commands and either transmit the copy over a telephone modem or send a floppy disk to a typesetter.

For school districts that have not been able to afford typesetting their publications, modern technology could make it an affordable option.

Working through Negotiations

Many school districts must produce printed contracts for each employee affected by new contract language. Secretaries type the initial version of the agreement, send the typed copy to printers, read, proof, and so on. The per hour costs of administrators, attorneys, and secretaries are all involved in the final production steps as each reads composer's proofs. Even the best composer averages one typographical error per page of typeset copy. Correcting errors once copy is typeset costs more than correcting copy on a computer screen in-house. Locating errors is important, since one error could damage delicate negotiations.

Using microcomputers in-house can eliminate the need for everyone to proofread typeset copy and ensures more accuracy in the final version of a contract. With electronic transfers from one microcomputer to another, words can be printed in the final document as people agree to them. With good word processing software, you can compose the final document on the screen and have multiple copies of the final document printed out for all the people involved.

Substantial savings accrue because there is no duplication of the original typing effort. More savings occur because there is no need to proofread typeset copy against the original copy. One person who is handling the final production can and should check for any problems that may have occurred during transmission, but that is all. The ultimate savings are, of course, that you are decreasing the chances and costs of errors because you are proofing and correcting at an earlier stage.

Telecommunications

Our strength as educators and communicators comes from having access to timely information and being able to distribute it in the best and fastest way possible to the people who need to know. Telecommunications provides this service.

The American Association of School Administrators and the National School Public Relations Association are just two of several national groups that have set up electronic information services. Subscribers to AASA ONLINE and NSPRA's ED-LINE have access, through their computers and the telephone lines, to a wide range of information that has direct impact on education.

In addition to these national networks, several states have set up networks to distribute important, timely information to their member schools or subscribers. In one state school districts that are signed up on a network through their state department of education receive test score information as it is processed. Schools that are not signed up have to wait longer for the information. In other states administrators are able to share information on legislative or contract negotiation issues.

On a day-to-day basis, electronic networks provide a valuable service to their subscribers. They furnish an avenue for gathering useful information for school managers and teachers and provide a forum for sharing ideas. Public relations administrators can use this information to develop newsletters, to post bulletin board notices, or route it to the appropriate people on the staff. Most districts and schools that are already part of a network would like to see all schools connected through an electronic information system.

A computer network can either tie into one of the national or state networks or stand alone. If you wish to connect your schools this way you should be aware of a few things. Taking care of a telecommunications network requires time and attention. The responsibility needs to be assigned to someone at each location. You also need to make sure that the people who use it receive adequate training and have the proper equipment. The information has to be timely and something that people cannot get as quickly elsewhere—or they won't bother to access it on the computer. To be effective within a school district, all the schools should be tied together with an appropriate type of microcomputer.

As part of your planning process, consider assigning a person to work with a school district that is already using a system. Once that person is fully trained and ready to go, he or she should probably train individuals in each school, if all the schools are tied into the system.

The potential for instant communications through computer networks is astounding. Some business offices are already taking advantage of this potential. The equipment allows for an instant exchange of ideas and information. Messages can be relayed to one or more people by directing them to their computer screens. No longer do you have to spend time trying to get someone on the phone or dictating and sending memos through a routing system. If you need to distribute information regarding a hot topic for the next board meeting to all principals, you can send it at one time via computer to all of them. They can also send you data as it is available for press conferences, board meetings, and so on. The system avoids busy signals and commands the attention of the computer user every time the machine is turned on—if a message is waiting. Once you have realized the power and ease of these new communications methods, it's tough to go back to the old ways.

Cable

Communities are fast becoming wired for cable television. Superstations challenge local broadcasters. As satellites bring new programming and new choices to television audiences, media experts tell us that the mass media are becoming "demassified."

As cable decisions are made in each community, school systems should be sure to get a piece of the action. Public access channels make it possible for schools, colleges and universities, and other public institutions to communicate information and events into thousands of homes.

How can schools make the best use of cable television?

■ Get involved in early discussions of cable in your community and maintain access.

■ Delegate responsibility for feeding the cable system to personnel who have the time and expertise to handle it.

■ Decide how you will program the time you have available on your public access channel.

■ Get the equipment you need. You will probably want cameras, switchers, audio equipment, lighting facilities, and studio space. Studio space and equipment are often already available in a high school or in the central office.

■ Involve staff and students in the production of programs.

■ Promote programs you have scheduled for your public access channel.

■ Always look for ways to improve your programs. Viewers flipping from one channel to another will compare your programs to networks and other local programming.

Faced with the challenge of programming a cable channel, many school systems soon recognize that television simply devours programming. Here are some examples of programming presented by school cable channels.

■ *News and information*, using a character generator. A character generator is very much like an electronic typewriter. Using this device, schools can present an electronic newsletter. Content might include news items, calendar information, and facts about the schools.

■ *Interviews*. One of the easiest types of programming to present is the interview. But doing the interview well and keeping the program exciting takes skill on the part of both interviewer and guest. Some programs feature several interviews in a magazine format in order to avoid exhausting a topic.

■ *School board meetings*. Some school systems fear covering board meetings live; they are concerned about grandstanding by board members, school personnel, and groups that come before the board to lobby for their cause. Many school systems have found that the regular presence of television makes board members more conscious of the efficient use of time and all the more conscious of how their actions might appear to a larger audience.

■ *School activities*. Classroom activities, science experiments, orchestra and chorus concerts, sports events, dance recitals, drama, and other school activities can provide excellent sources of programming and can bring school events to the entire community. Parents and students are proud to see themselves and their school recognized on television.

■ *Promotional*. Using a character generator, pre-taped announcements, and other means, a cable channel can be used to promote upcoming programs and school events.

Technology can now turn cable channels into interactive systems. Home instruction is available through television to students who are confined because of illness and who need reinforcement. The possibilities and challenges that cable presents must be taken seriously by all schools that have access to this important medium.

Teleconferencing

Bringing people together electronically through television, audio, or computer networks is becoming commonplace. While two-way visual links are the most expensive of these three approaches, the cost is likely to come down. Information highways will link schools within a school system and school systems within and among states. Satellite communication even makes it possible for students from several countries to be linked through television, audio, and computer hookups.

Instructional Television Fixed Service

Instructional Television Fixed Service (ITFS) systems provide schools with the capability to use low-power transmission to link schools and homes. Using microwave, a system carries for up to 50 miles. FCC licenses are required for these channels. Schools have only begun to use the potential of this system for forming audio and visual networks. Low-powered translator stations are also sometimes established to extend television signals to sites that may be beyond the reach of normal television broadcasting stations.

ITFS is now being used for much more than delivering courses or courseware to students. A number of states have developed networks to encourage courseware delivery for teachers. School systems often work in tandem with colleges and universities in these efforts.

The Future is Now

Picture yourself in your office at 3 p.m. It's been a busy day and your "to do" list still screams for attention. You and your secretary get together and discuss what needs to be done.

By 4 p.m., and using your internal and external computer network, you have:

- Sent a memo to all principals regarding a new regulation disseminated by the state department of education
- Made a plane reservation for the speech you have to give Monday
- Performed a literature search to obtain some data you needed for the speech
- Surveyed the principals to get their input on a controversial topic scheduled for tomorrow's board meeting
- Made the changes on a negotiated contract so that all affected employees will have individual copies within 48 hours
- Notified the superintendent of some media requests for interviews this evening about the closing of one of the elementary schools.

Videotape and Disc

An increasing number of school systems are using videotape to tell a school's story. In some cases, a video program replaces institutional slide presentations. Because video monitors are generally smaller than screens used for showing slides, more than one video monitor is often needed for a larger audience. When using video, lighting should be appropriate, shots should be well composed, and those featured should be knowledgeable and stimulating. Program length should not exceed the interesting material that you want to present.

Video disc presents increasing opportunities for interactive communication, especially in learning programs. A video disc player can be connected to a computer, making it possible for students to see a visual portrayal of an event or activity, followed by questions and reinforcement.

An Information Production System

One of the primary functions of a school district's communications program is producing news releases and disseminating information to the media. Microcomputers with appropriate software can increase the efficiency of performing these tasks and can add methods of distribution.

School districts generate many announcements for the media: school opening and closing dates, spring vacation dates, and other calendar information. Using today's technology, public relations directors can file the basic releases on a computer disc and update them appropriately. The more sophisticated user and system could maintain a file of names and addresses that can be updated easily. It is also possible to transmit releases over a telephone line directly to a newsroom's computer with the proper equipment. Many newspapers and radio stations are already set up to receive and send such transmissions, and more are converting their operations every day.

A microcomputer's ability to personalize form letters turns mail that would be thrown on a pile into mail that is read. When people receive a personalized letter, the message of the letter is strengthened and the credibility of the information soars. Consider the effect of a personalized letter containing details of the school budget, or the impact that is made when parents of graduates receive a letter from the superintendent thanking them for 13 years of support and reminding them that schools provide services for people 18 and over, too.

Tabulating Surveys

Community and issues surveys are an integral part of communications programs. Many districts have had to call in consultants to tabulate the data in the past. With the software now available for microcomputers, information can be entered and converted into spreadsheets, pie charts, and graphs. Many microcomputers are able to handle large quantities of data and conduct all sorts of computations with the proper software. This feature can be very helpful in preparing presentations for the school board or community.

Some educators have taken a leap forward from simply working out survey data. For example, after surveying a community on adult education courses, an administrator could send personalized letters to the 15 people who said they would like a course in "Latin for Left-handers." Ironically, the computer, branded by some people for being an impersonal machine, creates the possibility of a personalized approach in mass communication.

Determining Equipment Needs

We have referred to the need to have the proper equipment and software. Before you make the move into today's technology, most experts recommend that you study your needs, assign someone specifically to do the necessary research, and talk with other people who have already been there before you buy anything. The market for microcomputers and their various options changes a great deal from one month to the next. There are, however, certain basic components that most people end up buying. They are:

■ A microcomputer with sufficient RAM (internal memory system) to handle a broadbased spreadsheet program for tabulating surveys. The RAM of a machine is the heart of its ability to perform computations. If your needs will require a great deal of keyboarding, the comfort of the keyboard and the screen size are also important factors.

■ If the computer is going to replace a typewriter system, you will need a letter quality printer. Don't shortchange yourself here. If you buy well, the printer can be used to produce camera-ready copy for school publications and form letters as well as produce mailing labels.

■ For telecommunications (communicating through an electronic network) you will need a telephone modem. A modem provides the hookup between your computer and the phone system, which then ties into another computer. Many of the new micros have internal modems, which means that to hookup to a phone line, you just plug the telephone jack into the computer. Along with a modem you also need a telecommunications software package—again many of the newer micros include this software in their operating systems. If not, you will have to purchase it because you need the program so your computer can communicate with another one.

■ Software changes as often as computers. Companies and individuals work constantly to upgrade and modify their software programs so that they are more efficient and user friendly. When you buy a microcomputer, you will purchase as part of the initial investment a basic operating system. With many microcomputers, this is called the Disk Operating System (DOS). Either as part of that or as a separate package you will probably want a word processing program, a data base management program, an accounting program, and a telecommunications program to perform all the different types of procedures we have recommended.

12

Issues

Management

We're tired of surprises. ... Can't we predict these things will happen?
Why weren't we in a leadership position to take advantage of this
issue? It's always their agenda, never ours!

We live in a society driven by issues. Those issues often flow from special interest groups made up of people who either want to force change or keep it from happening. Often, these groups become highly organized and adept at raising issues.

Several years ago, professional educators could comfortably ignore tax credits. Now the issue commands attention. "Merit pay won't work," some educators said, and that was that. Now, many school systems have implemented or are considering merit plans in response to public pressure.

As a result, some schools have started looking seriously at how leading businesses make use of issues management techniques. Whether a school system adopts a formal issues management process or not, those who provide leadership should become more aware of issues management. Its techniques can be applied whenever appropriate to help a school system manage its position on important issues.

Issues Management—What Is It?

An *issue* is a trend or condition, internal or external, that may, does, or will affect the successful accomplishment of your objectives.

The term issues management may be somewhat misleading, since it is not always possible to manage an issue. Rather, issues management allows you to manage your position more effectively on an issue. In an effective issues management program, you will be involved in setting the agenda on the issue rather than simply responding to everyone else's agenda. Through an effective issues management program, educational leaders can become more proactive on behalf of education.

Spotting Issues As They Emerge

Every organization is faced with basically three types of issues:
■ *Critical Issues.* These issues command attention now!

99

- *Ongoing Issues.* These issues will always be with us. How much time and attention they take might vary from year to year or month to month. For example, the budget is an ongoing issue.
- *Emerging Issues.* These issues are just appearing on the horizon.

Educational leaders should develop systems that make it possible for them to spot issues as they emerge, before they are fully formed and sides are drawn. Getting a handle on an issue early in its life gives an organization the opportunity to shape the issue or to deal with it in its early stages. Often, when an issue reaches a meeting of the school board, state legislature, or another level of government, the school system is placed in a position of damage control. School leaders at this point may have lost the latitude to shape the issue.

Issues management is an important part of a sound public relations program. In fact, issues management is only one part of a planned, continuous program of communication. A well-organized program makes it possible for an organization to:
- Identify issues early
- Address issues articulately and in a timely fashion
- Understand those who support or oppose certain positions on the issues
- Shape issues in a way that will contribute to good education
- Adopt or even work to defeat certain positions on issues.

An issues management program also creates channels for communication with staff and community and builds coalitions of individuals, groups, and organizations that share a concern about individual issues.

The Issues Management Process

There are seven basic steps in the issues management process:
1. issue identification
2. analysis
3. prioritization
4. strategy development
5. strategy implementation
6. ongoing evaluation and course corrections
7. post-mortem or evaluation

Issue Identification

Issues should be identified early before they become surrounded by strong special interest groups. When issues become viable, they are usually adopted by an individual, elected official, bureaucrat, or other more "official" organization. Once adopted, the issue often moves forward to the point that a decision-making official or body must take action to resolve it. Of course, it is possible for you or your organization to capture and become an authority on an appropriate issue.

Issues can be identified in several ways. Analyze carefully public and staff opinion polls and listen to feedback from key communicators who participate in meetings and special events. Some astute issues managers conduct regular "think-tank" sessions with key groups of staff and community representatives to identify emerging issues. Focus groups could also be formed to explore the issue horizon. Many organizations develop scanning systems to help identify issues that first appear in the media.

Many major corporations and school districts, using issues management techniques, have identified as many as 200-300 issues that may or will impact on an organization's ability to meet its objectives. For some, the list changes, sometimes daily, depending on how volatile the environment may be.

Once an issue is identified, someone in the organization is assigned to "own" the issue, to become its best expert. That person develops an issue paper, collects all supporting materials on the issue, tracks it, and updates the issue paper. He or she keeps the issue manager apprised of changes and recommends, when appropriate, how the issue might be handled.

By using microcomputer and word processing technology, it is possible to keep a record of all issues on your list and use as many experts as you wish to help track each issue. In many organizations that either choose not to use electronic technology or decide to limit the scope of issues they follow, five to seven issues are selected each year for development of management plans. The limitation of this approach is that it usually focuses only on the "squeaky-wheel" issues and may leave little room for a proactive approach.

Once the best expert prepares an issue paper, it should be reviewed and approved by an appropriate division or department head charged with responsibility for dealing with that particular type of issue. Only after review and approval should the issue be moved to an issue management task force.

Writing an Issue Paper

An issue paper should be kept short—one or two pages. It includes:
- A clear statement of the issue.
- The impact on the district in some measurable terms.
- The position of the district or those being considered.
- Issue analysis—what does it mean; why; background; actions.
- Critical follow-up date(s)—what will happen next and when?
- Key contact(s)—who keeps the files and records on this issue?
- Other resources and biographical references, files.

Sample Issue Paper:

Category: Board of Education
Classification: Districtwide

Record No.:
Current to: 6/23/—

Priority:*
Type: C

Title: Desegregation Appeal

Summary: The Board of Education voted to appeal the Desegregation Court Order issued in 19—. The district's position is to follow court decisions to the letter of the law. The outcome of the current appeal will be no different.

Impact: All departments of the district are on a standby basis in order to implement the decision of the court as related to the appeal.

Position: The district has taken the position in the past that it will execute all court decisions in good faith, both in spirit and to the letter. If the district finds that it still has good reason to appeal, the current decision will be followed until a subsequent ruling is made.

Followup Date: 8/15/—

Explanation: Check status. Attorneys have indicated that the decision related to the appeal may occur near December 1, 19—.

Background: The school district has been involved in court cases related to desegregation since 1956. Each decision reached was implemented in good faith, and generally appealed either by the district, the plaintiffs, or both. The Board of Education is anxious to get the district out of court, but it voted to appeal based on the belief that the district has desegregated to the fullest extent, with the low percentage of Anglo students remaining in the district and that the desegregation order of 19——, which changed boundaries for Thomas Jones, Etheridge, and Adams high schools, resulted in unnecessary changes to the student makeups of already naturally desegregated schools.

It is hoped that this appeal will be the last and that the district can devote all of its time and money after this decision to building a quality educational system.

Contact: Ext. 200, Key Administrator
Contact: Ext. 381, District Expert
Bibliography: Order of U.S. District Court of April 7, 19—.

Some issues trackers, such as John Naisbitt, author of *Megatrends*, use a technique called "content analysis." Here is how the process might work in a school system:

■ Make an inventory of publications currently read by key staff, department heads, or community members. Add to that list any publications that represent special interest groups or political organizations.

■ Once the list is complete, assign one person to be a scanner for each publication. That is, he or she reads every issue and identifies articles or references that may indicate an emerging issue or add new information to issues already being tracked.

■ The process might extend to monitoring radio and television news and public service broadcasts and attending meetings of key community groups.

Analysis and Priority Setting

The task force, representing the superintendent or other top manager, is responsible for analyzing the issue, setting priorities, and determining the district's position. In some cases, the position might require sanction from the board of education.

When an organization is faced with a multitude of issues, it is important to set priorities. Priorities are usually set on the basis of how important it is for the district to manage a strong position or to deal effectively with the issue. Priorities are based on:

■ *Time.* When will this issue need to be resolved? When will it affect us?

■ *Probability.* How likely is it to affect us or to happen? A 50-50 chance? A 90 percent chance?

■ *Significance.* How important is it in comparison with other issues?

■ *Impact.* How significant will the impact be on the school system, its mission, goals, and objectives? How will it affect education for students? The task force might agree that the issue will be of high, medium, or low impact.

The task force reviews each issue in relation to all others to set priorities. All issues are weighted one to five in terms of priority. Once the top issues are identified, the staff develops a strategic plan to help implement a district's position or otherwise manage the issue in such a way that high quality education will benefit.

Strategy Development and Implementation

Let's assume we have determined that computer equity is an issue. This means that we are concerned about the availability of computers for low income students to use for homework, data-library searches, and so on. The issue is a priority to your district. A briefing paper was prepared by the division of instruction and referred to the task force. As a top priority, a strategy is needed to respond to the issue and to manage the district's position. The district has decided its position is to develop a program to ensure that access to computers will be equally available to all students and that a program to implement the position will go to the board of education in three months.

The issues management task force refers the issue to an ad hoc task force to develop an issues management strategy. The strategy consists of two parts—the development of a plan for handling the availability of computers to all students and the communications component needed to implement the plan. The communications plan needs to include both media and interpersonal communications activities.

The strategy is reviewed by the issues management task force and approved (or modified) for implementation. As a strategy is implemented, it is essential to monitor it. Course corrections may be required based on the evaluation and feedback received.

Post Mortem

After a strategy has been completed, the task force should evaluate it and determine its impact on other priorities. We learn from our mistakes. Who helped us in our coalition? Who did we leave out? What were our strengths and weaknesses? Whether we win or lose, a post mortem is essential.

13

Conducting

Campaigns

Conducting a school campaign requires plenty of dedicated people, energy, and planning. It's vital that you rely on what your research says, whether you're trying to gain support for a bond election to build a new school; get the community to support a tax levy, or muster the needed clout to prod the town council for support.

Many well-intentioned campaigns prove unsuccessful because they are put together quickly by officials who ignore information on how the community accepts or rejects ideas. Other campaigns designed to improve the schools and community don't make it because they are disjointed, raise doubts, and lack the kind of leadership necessary to show long-term results.

Other campaigns fail because an administrator with a little bit of knowledge about public relations tries to do it all, using only one method of communication. For example, some school officials who enjoy an excellent relationship with the media will emphasize newspapers, radio, and television, forgetting that face-to-face communication plays a major role in campaigns.

Face-To-Face Communication

Researchers who studied how new ideas are accepted tell us that the mass media and other one-way communications work during the early information stages, when people are getting to know about an idea or a need. Those same researchers, however, explain that when people are ready to decide whether they are for or against something or whether they will buy a product or an idea, face-to-face communication often makes the difference.

Campaigns Must Capitalize on Planning

Too often school boards and school administrators expect a campaign to overcome years of communications neglect in a school-community relations program. It does not and cannot. Taxpayers who have been ignored for years seldom support needs identified by school leaders who suddenly contact them.

Here are some questions to ask before embarking on a campaign:

■ *Is our philosophy to tell or to persuade?*

Do you feel that it is the responsibility of school officials to present factually the needs only and then get out of the way? Or do you feel that it is the job of school leaders to explain the needs in a dynamic way, showing the impact on education? Which method would be more effective?

■ *Has the community been represented in studying the need?*

When community members other than just school board members are involved in evaluating solutions to a problem, their support is a powerful component in a campaign. When advisory committees study the need for a new building or a tax levy, the need is received more favorably by the community. Asking for the support of a committee after the levy has been set or the building planned by a select few board members seldom merits enthusiastic support.

■ *What is the history of similar campaigns?*

Often board members and administrators fail to capitalize on experiences gained from previous campaign efforts. Before starting any major campaign, seek the counsel of key community and school supporters who have played major roles in earlier campaigns. Check how various precincts voted in the past. Also, do some homework. Go through back issues of local newspapers to see which issues—if any—captured the attention of voters.

■ *Is it possible to develop a position that the board can support unanimously?*

When a school board is split on a campaign issue, the chance for approval is appreciably reduced. Before placing the board in a split position, determine if there is a way to make subtle modifications that will move the board toward approving a compromise position unanimously. Each board member claims a following in the community. Is it possible to overcome the followings that board members opposed to the issue will bring to the polls?

■ *Have school officials gained support of the appropriate community governing bodies?*

Working with government officials at all levels provides political punch when needed. These people also have to care about public reactions to taxes, and keeping them informed regularly about school needs, successes, and challenges is smart management.

No one governing body in a community should be surprised by the actions of another when those actions have an impact on the other's area of responsibility.

■ *Have students and staff been involved in studying the need? Have both groups been invited to offer suggestions?*

People who get their information about schools from people who attend them or work in them tend to support school needs more than people who use other sources for their information. Keeping staff members informed on how a special need will help people learn better makes it easier for them to spread the word in the community. However, a school should avoid any kind of coercion to get staff and students to support issues.

106

■ *Has a budget been set to conduct a campaign?*

A campaign with good ideas and no money to implement them will usually fall short of its goals. Yet, many states prohibit schools from spending taxpayer money to encourage people to vote for spending more taxpayer money.

To allow money to be raised and spent for school campaign services, many public spirited citizens have formed campaign committees. Working outside the official school family, they are permitted to conduct a "let's win" campaign.

■ *Has the right primary spokesperson been chosen to explain the needs to the community?*

It's vital that the most credible communicator on the school management team be chosen for this job. That might be the superintendent or another key administrator. It's also possible that the primary spokesperson be someone outside the school management team, perhaps a highly respected community leader. Undoubtedly, a number of people will address the issue publicly; however, the primary spokesperson will have the necessary information, good judgment, and credibility to address any concerns as they arise.

Develop the Plan

After asking and answering key questions, school officials should develop plans for the campaign. Paramount is the fact that people can accomplish only so much when they are expected to maintain their regular responsibilities.

One of the first steps of the plan is to determine which audiences are most important and how they can be reached. (See chapter three for more on planning.)

By tapping the research findings noted earlier in this chapter, develop the early informational stages of the campaign. This includes providing news releases, newsletters, and other one-way information. Remember, be forthright when presenting facts and needs. An overzealous supporter can ruin a campaign.

Get Facts Straight

Be sure of facts and communicate them in writing to all who will represent the campaign committee. It's imperative that everyone play from the same deck of cards.

If media representatives ask questions that don't have immediate answers, do some homework and get the correct answers. Don't guess. People will assume the worst if a school official is found providing incorrect information.

Use figures that are easy to understand. Use common words and graphic examples. Be clear. For example: Telling residents that a new school will cost $18.2 million doesn't communicate much to the average taxpayer. But explaining that the additional average tax cost will be 18 cents per day tells the story.

Avoid the temptation to provide unwanted details. Don't, for example, show a floor plan of the building because the architect thinks it's a good idea. Most taxpayers don't care to read blueprints, and those who do seldom care about details. Of course, make those plans available on request. If the floor plan is an issue for voters, publish it.

The same philosophy should apply when seeking support for major curricular changes. The lay person doesn't necessarily need to know the intricacies of affective and cognitive domains. Simply explain that the new approach to teaching reading should help students learn better. Document the decision with information gathered from other schools that have used the approach, and keep the explanations concise.

Get People Involved

Q: *How do you think a retired carpenter, age 66, will vote on a school tax issue? He lives on a fixed income.*
A: *Against it—most people would say.*

Let's try the same question after a variable has been introduced. The carpenter visits his local elementary school four times a year to speak in various classes. He also judges a woodshop class competition in the high school.

Do you feel the answer might be different under these circumstances?

Research shows that people who have been in the schools for any reason during the year preceding an election involving school funds tend to support the needs more than others do.

The implications are clear. School officials should encourage community groups to use the schools. They should expand adult education and community education programs, and they should implement techniques that invite taxpayers to visit and get involved in their schools.

Speak to Service Organizations

When people are uncertain how they feel about an innovation or tax need, they often look to peers for advice and direction. Many respect

---

Caution: How Not To Do It

The school district newsletter focusing on the proposed new building was due to come out in a month. The school staff wanted to show the need without saying, "vote yes," which was prohibited by state law.

What they did: A photographer was hired to take photos of the crowded library. The fact was that the library was indeed overcrowded just about every period. However, when the photographer arrived, the library was almost empty. To solve the photographer's problem, an administrator told hundreds of students from a number of classes to go to the library and make it look crowded for a picture.

One of the pictures was used in the newsletter. The students told their friends, parents, and neighbors that the picture was staged. Credibility was destroyed. The referendum was clobbered on election day.

people who belong to the same service organizations they do; thus, presentations made to groups such as the Jaycees or Kiwanis can pay off with public support. Not only can you make your case with the members, but you may be able to rely on their public support during a campaign. You could list their support in newspaper ads or flyers; perhaps they would even be interested in contributing to or sponsoring an endorsement ad.

This approach also capitalizes on the research finding that people accept or reject new ideas or proposals based primarily on face-to-face communication.

Organize Coffee Klatches

When planning techniques that work, don't overlook the often used and very effective "coffee klatch." This approach works because it allows face-to-face communication to play a key role in decision making about innovations. Talking to a school official and/or a citizens committee member and getting answers to questions in person is much more effective than only getting answers from a brochure. In addition, the people who sponsor the coffee klatches tend to become more ardent supporters of the schools and their needs.

Identify Yes Voters

Perhaps the biggest single factor that affects the outcome at the polls is identifying "yes" voters, getting them registered, and making sure they vote.

If this reads like a typical political campaign, it is. School officials can learn a great deal from people who have been getting the vote out for years. Again, the work generally must be done by a citizens committee not financed by the schools.

Identifying Yes, No, and Don't Know Voters

Many political campaigns have developed various strategies for contacting and using the yes vote. Here's one way to do it:

Committee members, other concerned citizens, and special block workers are all assigned specific areas to canvass. They all ask one question: "We're here to gain support for the new school building that's being voted on. We need you to help us call on others to encourage them to vote 'yes.' Will you help?" The answers fall into these categories:

—Sure, I'd like to help (this occurs about once in every 200 responses).

—Gee, I'd like to help, but I'm too busy (chances are this is a yes voter).

—No, we don't need more taxes (clearly, not a yes voter).

A card is prepared on each voter. Those expected to vote yes are prime candidates for reminder phone calls, child watching assistance, etc. Of course, those who indicated an interest in helping should be followed up with requests for their services. Follow-up on all positive responses is essential.

Marketing Communication

Marketing and Public Relations

The definition for marketing that seems most universal is: everything you do to sell your product or services. And, while some people feel we should market the schools, we must remember that the public doesn't have to buy the school system. The public already owns it and continues to pay for it with hard-earned tax dollars.

Nevertheless, school systems do have products and services available for purchase. Many schools offer community and adult education programs, curriculum materials that are available to other districts, and bond and finance issues that need to be accepted by voters. In these and other cases, marketing techniques have a legitimate place in the overall communications effort of a school system. Problems can arise when school officials start calling their public relations efforts a marketing program. When that happens, community residents might feel that the schools are trying to sell them something rather than being responsive to educational needs.

Some people may feel that marketing is merely using billboards, bumper stickers, magazine ads, T-shirts, clever slogans, and assorted gimmicks to entice people to be interested in and buy a product or service. Marketing professionals know it is much more.

The Four P's of Marketing

Traditionally marketing has included the four P's—product, packaging, promotion, and pricing. Some have recently included a fifth P, positioning—determining where the product or service fits among competing or similar services.

As the number of school-aged people dropped and as tax credit talk increased, many school officials sought a plan to attract students to the public schools. They were often concerned about the recruitment efforts of private schools. Some felt they were developing marketing plans; others referred to what they were doing as a public relations plan with a marketing component.

Getting Yes Voters Registered

For years school officials counted on parents of school-aged children to provide enough positive votes to approve school voting issues. Now with fewer than 65 percent of the voters having children in many school systems, it's vital that all who might vote "yes" be encouraged to register. A number of case studies show that the number of people voting "no" on school issues seems to remain fairly constant. The solution is to get more yes voters registered and to the polls.

Although it's only right that all voters should receive information about school needs, the time and effort invested trying to convert no voters is usually better spent getting yes voters out to vote. This is especially true in school districts where fewer than 25 percent of the registered voters turn out for school elections.

Two Special Yes Vote Groups

Investing time and effort to capture the interest and votes of 18-to-21-year-olds and absentee ballot candidates could make the difference in

Both public relations and marketing are research-based. Both demand knowledge of the consumer. Both require a knowledge of what people know and don't know about a product or service, and both are concerned with attitudes, but public relations is a communications program and marketing is a selling program.

Quality Product is Essential

In any public relations effort, chances for success are nonexistent if the product or service is inferior. Actually, the best way to guarantee a bad product's demise is to advertise it.

Both marketing and public relations work to ensure quality. With schools, a product or service must meet legitimate community needs. In the long run, images are built on quality and can't be established with a billboard or button. A carefully planned program, however, can include as part of an ongoing public relations effort vehicles aimed at making educational programs more responsive to community needs coupled with gaining support.

Positioning the Schools

Positioning the schools could be one of the greatest future challenges facing educators. As more nontraditional students seek education, as more older citizens have time for courses, and as technological changes demand retraining for new skills, community residents are seeking direction and leadership from educators. Administrators who seize these opportunities will position the schools as the learning place in the community—the one place to go for quality educational services of several types.

Marketing communication can be an important element in an effective public relations program. However, it is not a substitute for a sound public relations program, nor can it be used as a substitute for improving education.

---

your campaign. The 18-to-21-year-olds appreciate being wooed—perhaps for the first time—as voters. People in this age group are seldom affected by an increased property tax and recognize school needs since most of them only recently completed school in your district. An alumni association is a natural organizer for communications aimed at this select group.

Young voters—be they away at college or in the service—seldom think to use an absentee ballot. Yet, a number of school elections claimed victory because of lopsided positive results from absentee voters.

Again, the alumni association can be instrumental in gaining this special support. The association can send a letter addressed to the parents of former students or those in the service and ask that the enclosed, stamped letter be mailed to the graduates, wherever they are. The letter explains how to request an absentee ballot and urges the reader to support the school issue. The payoff for the effort is consistently excellent.

---

*For an excellent collection of winning case studies and ideas that worked for other school officials who conducted campaigns, see "You Can Win at the Polls." This practical kit is available from the National School Public Relations Association, 1501 Lee Highway, Arlington, VA 22209.

Get the Vote Out

The day before an election, the committee should be sure calls are made to all who are listed as potential yes voters to remind them of voting hours and places. Research shows that 15 percent of voters who wanted to support school needs say they forgot to vote on election day. (Note: Organize this effort well; too many phone calls can alienate voters.)

On election day check off the names of those who vote. If you use this strategy, be sure your people are aware of the laws requiring that they be a certain distance from the polls. As the time left diminishes to a few hours, have poll watchers call those who haven't voted to see if they need a ride or need babysitters for their children.

After a Campaign

After a campaign, conduct research to see what seemed to work and what didn't. Make recommendations for next time. Thank all who helped—whether the campaign was successful or not. That little touch of class might make it easier to elicit support in another campaign.

If the campaign produced a new school or a budget that allowed some new programs or community acceptance of an innovative program, don't forget to issue progress reports on how the investment is paying off. Give credit to the community.

For example, if the budget approval provided another full-time speech therapist, tell taxpayers at the end of the year that 22 students no longer have special problems. If the budget allowed a new reading program to be initiated, share reading test score improvements. People like to feel they made the right decision.

Thematic Efforts

A thematic effort can gain support for high quality education and help citizens and staff understand better how important education is to our society. A short, rhythmic, and easy-to-remember theme serves as a consensus statement.

Too often, organizations try to use slogans rather than thematic efforts. A thematic effort is undergirded by sound objectives that lead to improvements. A slogan is generally an attention-getter used to sell a product. However, one automaker recently announced that, "At Nissan, quality is more than a slogan." The same should be true in the schools.

Some themes used by schools include: Quest for Quality, Getting Better for Kids, Champions of Learning, and Public Education: A Sound Investment in America. Whatever the theme, staff and community should understand it, feel good about it, and be stirred by it. It should create, in the best sense possible, a bandwagon for high quality education.

14

Evaluation

From a public relations standpoint, one of the best things you can do is ensure a sound evaluation system for all school programs and personnel. The public has a right to know that its tax money is spent wisely, that people and programs are working well, and that problems are identified and corrected.

The public relations program of a school system should be evaluated on a regular basis, just as other programs are. However, a system's foundation for success is often based on how it evaluates all personnel and programs. For example:

■ Are all school employees evaluated, at least in part, on their communications performance? Do communications responsibilities exist in job descriptions and do communications objectives exist for secretaries, principals, teachers, custodians, bus drivers, food service personnel, school board members, the superintendent, and others?

■ Do all school programs contain a public relations component to ensure that they are understood and that reactions to them are heard?

■ Does the public relations program have policy support, and does it have the people, funds, equipment, and encouragement it needs to be successful?

Four key purposes of public relations evaluations are:

■ To determine whether a program is achieving its objectives

■ To determine if the results are meeting the expectations for the investment

■ To make decisions about continuing, modifying, dropping, or adopting new public relations activities

■ To bring greater visibility to the accomplishments of the public relations program.

A sound system of evaluation can help you determine if your public relations program is adequately funded and staffed to accomplish what the school system expects it to do. It can help measure how well staff members feel they are informed. It can help you determine behavior or attitude changes among staff and community to assist you in setting targets for improving the situation.

School public relations programs often are evaluated based on whether the school district is receiving its share of good press. But news media relations are part of a much larger whole.

Methods exist to assist schools in evaluating their public relations efforts. Since attitudes change based on events far beyond the control of local schools, the school public relations program cannot necessarily be held accountable for all changes in community attitudes. However, if a public relations program can help the system understand better the attitude change that is taking place, then it has served the schools well in that particular realm.

Guiding Principles of Evaluation

Here are some basic public relations evaluation principles developed by the National School Public Relations Association (NSPRA):

■ Practice both formative and summative evaluation.

Evaluate public relations activities while they are underway so that you can make course corrections to improve the activity (formative evaluation). Also, periodically review the impact of your total program (summative) and tie it to the planning process in developing future programs (formative).

■ Strive to go beyond just the traditional public relations evaluation methods of measuring news clippings, meeting deadlines, and attending special events and begin measuring levels of understanding, attitudes, opinions, and behavior changes among targeted publics.

Evaluative questions can be added to regular school or district opinion polls. Information can also be gleaned from issues surveys if a school system has established an issues management program.

Methods of Evaluation

Three major systematic approaches to evaluation are: (1) a program evaluation checklist; (2) communication audits; and (3) evaluating objectives.

Using An Evaluation Instrument

The National School Public Relations Association, in its guidebook *Evaluating Your School Public Relations Investment*, offers a public relations program evaluation instrument. This checklist approach to evaluation asks questions such as:

■ Do you have a public relations board policy to demonstrate the board's commitment to public relations?

■ Are administrative procedures in place, and is the ultimate public relations responsibility delegated to one person?

■ Is the public relations function staffed and financed adequately?

■ Does the public relations official have immediate access to the superintendent?

■ Is the public relations official a member of the top administrative team?

■ Is the public relations official one of the first to know of major happenings in the school district?

■ Is a two-way internal public relations program in place?

■ Does the public relations program identify target audiences and develop a plan to meet the communication needs of these audiences?

- Does the external public relations program employ a variety of communication techniques?
- Is a crisis communication plan available?
- Does the public relations person become involved in long range planning?
- Does the public relations program analyze feedback from internal and external publics?

By answering these questions and others, an administrator can begin to identify strengths and weaknesses in the public relations program's organization.

Communication Audit

Another systematic approach to evaluation is the communication audit, an analysis of your school district's internal and external communications. An audit is designed to take a snapshot of your system's communication needs, policies, activities, capabilities, and programs. It involves staff and community leaders and leads to a set of recommendations from a communication expert.

A comprehensive audit uncovers communication gaps and suggests:
- Priorities for short and long term goals
- Themes/issues to be emphasized
- Priority list of publics
- Ways to determine the community's pulse on key issues
- Communication methods that are working
- New communication methods that are warranted
- A measuring stick for future evaluations.

Many skilled public relations professionals in school systems provide this service for individual schools and build monitoring techniques to trace the effectiveness of districtwide programs. While an outside audit can provide a dispassionate look at a school system's public relations efforts, the recommendations of the person doing the audit must be placed in the context of the local district. People inside the district may know things that simply don't show up in the audit.

A school district communication audit follows five basic steps:
- *Researching:* reviewing the current program and data on the school and community
- *Finding out what "we" think:* talking to key management and assessing the school district's strengths and weaknesses in instruction, management, and public relations
- *Finding out what "they" think:* going to key internal and external publics and seeking their opinions on strengths and weaknesses in instruction, management, and public relations
- *Evaluating the difference between what "we" and "they" said:* developing a public relations balance sheet of assets, liabilities, strengths, and weaknesses
- *Recommending how to close the gaps uncovered in the audit.*

Audits are sometimes completed by outside experts who have experience in working with school districts. An audit often analyzes feedback and recommends new public relations initiatives for the school district. It can create new perspectives on public relations among school administrators and employees. A good audit points out the need for a systematic approach and helps everyone realize that publicity alone or one-shot activities do not constitute a sound public relations program. Many high grade programs include on an ongoing basis most of the methods used in an audit.

Evaluating Public Relations Objectives

Performance-based evaluation techniques in public relations are used with increasing frequency. Measuring attitudes and opinions of selected audiences is an important evaluation technique. Opinion surveys, advisory groups, and other methods can be used to obtain significant data.

To a great extent, public relations objectives should be connected to the overall objectives of the school or school system. In addition public relations plans and activities should be a part of every program.

One caution in measuring objectives is that measuring results must not be allowed to interfere inordinately with a smoothly operating public relations office. Evaluating public relations objectives must become part of the office's routine or it may not be worth the extra effort. The evaluation system should not be so time consuming that there is little time left for the public relations effort. There are often ways to insert some evaluative questions into surveys or other feedback devices already planned for regular programs throughout the year.

Additional Evaluation Techniques

So far, we have focused on systematic approaches to evaluation. Other approaches may also be used depending on the sophistication of your public relations program.

The major thrust of all formal and informal efforts is *feedback*. We must listen carefully to our publics and remain close to those we serve.

Here is a list of useful evaluation tips and techniques. Some are more formal and expensive than others. If you choose to use informal techniques, just remember the fundamental premise: Bad information is worse than no information at all. Use informal feedback techniques only as an aid in indicating community and staff opinions.

Some techniques are:

■ Plot a grid to see how many of the targeted publics in your district you are reaching effectively (see page 30). Highly rated public relations programs reach targeted audiences with targeted messages. It is easy to mail the same newsletter to all audiences, but it is more difficult to tailor it to communicate specific messages to specific audiences.

■ Survey your community scientifically on various issues at least once a year. Hire an outside opinion research firm or establish your own scientific survey process, if possible. Make sure your process is scientific, or critics will easily discount your results. Attempt to couple evaluation questions with other surveys planned throughout the year.

■ Make evaluation postcards available in public spots throughout your community. Focus on issues on which you want opinions. The technique is informal and unscientific, but it provides valuable information.

■ Ask your switchboard operator or other clerical support staff members (if you have a decentralized phone system) to monitor issues, compliments, and complaints. This feedback can be helpful in evaluating and planning your public relations program.

- Seek feedback from parent-teacher organizations. Determine which activities they consider to be most effective and what ideas they suggest to strengthen communication with parents.

- Monitor call-in radio shows for comments about your schools.

- Keep a file of current correspondence and media editorials.

- Use various mailing lists you have—not just your newsletter readers—to ask a few pertinent questions. These lists might include staff people who get your internal memos or advisory committee members with whom you try to keep in touch. Again, there may be little scientific validity to the results, but you'll get the idea if there's something seriously wrong.

Focus Groups and Survey Panels

An increasing number of organizations use focus groups as a non-scientific source of information and attitudes. Representatives of a target group come together to express themselves on questions that are part of a focused agenda. These focus groups often contain eight to 12 people.

While some organizations use focus groups to stay in touch, others rely on these important feedback groups to provide indications of concerns that might be tested later in more scientific surveys. In many cases, the focus group discussion begins by asking participants how they feel about an issue or program. Then the discussion moves to an exploration of how members of the group think others feel. A focus group can even assist in developing survey questions.

Ned Hubbell, veteran public relations consultant from Michigan and an advocate of focus groups, also suggests that schools consider the use of survey panels. These panels include people identified as opinion leaders in the community. Hubbell recommends a "reputational technique" for selecting members. Ask a number of knowledgeable people (newspaper editors, mayors, PTA leaders, etc.) what individuals most people listen to when it comes to schools. "These are the people whose opinions seem to count most when schools are discussed," Hubbell explains.

The names mentioned most often become candidates for a survey panel. Each member of the panel obtains essential information about the schools and receives a periodic questionnaire asking opinions about school issues. A typical question, according to Hubbell, might be, "If we handle this problem in this way, what could be the reactions or concerns?"

Survey panels can help a school system track changes in thinking. One caution: Hubbell adds that after a length of time, members of the panel may become so knowledgeable about the schools that they are atypical, no longer representative of most people on the street.

The form on page 118 reflects some typical questions from a building level survey of parents.

Sample Parent Opinion Survey

Dear Parent,

Please take time to respond to these comments. Your feelings are very important. We want to gather parent attitudes to help us set school goals and objectives. The results of this survey will be published in an upcoming newsletter and mailed to your home. Please place the completed survey in the box on the table in the center of the main gym. Thank you for participating.

My child is enrolled in ____ 7th grade, ____ 8th grade, ____ 9th grade, ____ SLIC, ____ PC.

Instructions: Please read each comment carefully. Answer the comment by circling the response with which you most agree. Please feel free to write your comments as well. They are helpful.

1. I am happy my child attends Smith Junior High.
   Yes   No   Other   Comment:

2. My child thinks Smith Junior High is a good school.
   Yes   No   Other   Comment:

3. Do you feel welcome when you visit this school?
   Yes   No   Other   Comment:

4. Are the school personnel helpful and courteous?
   Yes   No   Other   Comment:

5. I feel the teachers are helping my child attain a healthy self-concept.
   Yes   No   Other   Comment:

6. I feel the teachers are helping their students develop the ability to think.
   Yes   No   Other   Comment:

7. I feel the teachers are helping their students learn the fundamental skills.
   Yes   No   Other   Comment:

8. I feel the teachers are teaching skills that will help their students participate effectively in society.
   Yes   No   Other   Comment:

9. Are the principal and assistant principal easy to see and talk with?
   Yes   No   Other   Comment:

10. I feel this school provides adequate opportunity to students for exploring career education.
    Yes   No   Other   Comment:

11. Is the school keeping you informed about school activities?
    Yes   No   Other   Comment:

12. Do you read the school newsletter?   Yes   No
    What would you suggest be done to improve the newsletter?
    Yes   No   Other   Comment:

13. Do you feel the length of the school day is satisfactory?
    Yes   No   Other   Comment:

14. I feel this school provides students with experiences in leadership.
    Yes   No   Other   Comment:

15. I feel this school provides students with experiences in leadership.
    Yes   No   Other   Comment:

- Telephone residents to measure opinions and attitudes about issues on which your public relations program is currently focusing.

- Form a communications advisory group to meet on a scheduled basis to review communications programs and to give feedback and advice. Ask the group to advise you on long range concerns. A good advisory group can help provide a window on the community and the future.

Three Steps to Excellence

To improve public relations in a school district, you must do three things.

First you need to decide what the public relations program is supposed to accomplish. Goals and objectives should be appropriate and realistic.

Next, measure the impact of the public relations program and analyze whether it did what it was intended to do. What worked best? What did not work well, and why?

Finally, take what you learned from evaluation and use it to build a stronger public relations action plan for your district. Use feedback to make course corrections. The path to your school district's goals can be enhanced greatly by the public relations program.

To maintain an effective public relations effort, a school system must acknowledge it and take public pride in its success. It is, after all, the organization's connection with those it serves.

Whenever possible, weave an evaluation thread into every aspect of your public relations program. It's easy to show through careful evaluation that public relations does make a visible difference in the mission of your school district.

15

Public Relations

Resources

This book provides a variety of practical ideas. It's important, however, to know about other sources of public relations help.

The following list offers some books, periodicals, and associations that many administrators call on to help them communicate better.

In addition, many of the association and periodical publishers offer public relations workshops. State organizations can also be helpful.

A Theme for Your Schools ... Why and How. Arlington, Va.: American Association of School Administrators, 1984.

Bagin, Don; Gallagher, Don; and Kindred, Leslie W. *The School and Community Relations.* Englewood Cliffs, N.J.: Prentice-Hall, 1984.

Bernays, Edward L. *Crystallizing Public Opinion.* New York, N.Y.: Liveright Publishing Co., 1961.

Bernays, Edward L. *The Engineering of Consent.* Norman, Okla.: University of Oklahoma Press, 1956.

Brodinsky, Ben. *Building Morale, Motivating Staff.* Arlington, Va.: American Association of School Administrators, 1983.

Brodinsky, Ben. *Declining Enrollment ... Closing Schools.* Arlington, Va.: American Association of School Administrators, 1981.

Building Confidence in Education: A Practical Approach for Principals. Arlington, Va.: National Association of Secondary School Principals, 1982.

Building Public Confidence for your Schools. Arlington, Va.: National School Public Relations Association, 1978.

Center, Allen and Cutlip, Scott M. *Effective Public Relations.* Englewood Cliffs, N.J.: Prentice-Hall, 1982.

Chase, W. Howard. *Issue Management: Origins for the Future.* Stamford, Conn.: Issue Action Publications, 1984.

D'Aprix, Robert. *Communicating for Productivity.* New York, N.Y.: Harper & Row, 1982.

Evaluating Your School PR Investment. Arlington, Va.: National School Public Relations Association, 1984.

Goal Setting and Self Evaluation of School Boards. Arlington, Va.: American Association of School Administrators, 1980.

Grunig, James E. and Hunt, Todd. *Managing Public Relations.* New York, N.Y.: Holt, Rinehart and Winston, 1984.

Holding Effective Board Meetings. Arlington, Va.: American Association of School Administrators and National School Boards Association, 1984.

Hoyle, John; English, Fenwick; and Steffy, Betty. *Skills for Successful School Leaders.* Arlington, Va.: American Association of School Administrators, 1985.

Hymes, Donald L. *School Budgeting . . . Problems and Solutions.* Arlington, Va.: American Association of School Administrators, 1982.

Lesly, Philip. *Lesly's Public Relations Handbook.* Englewood, Cliffs, N.J.: Prentice-Hall, 1983.

Marx, Gary. *Building Public Confidence in our Schools.* Arlington, Va.: American Association of School Administrators, 1983.

Marx, Gary. *Radio: Your Publics Are Listening.* Washington, D.C.: National School Boards Association, 1976.

Neill, Shirley Boes, ed. *Planning for Tomorrow's Schools: Problems and Solutions.* Arlington, Va.: American Association of School Administrators, 1983.

New Voices on the Right: Impact on Schools. Arlington, Va.: National School Public Relations Association, 1982.

PR for School Board Members. Arlington, Va.: American Association of School Administrators, 1976.

You Can Win at the Polls: A Finance Campaign Kit. Arlington, Va.: National School Public Relations Association, 1980.

OTHER PUBLICATIONS

Amundson, Kristen. *Performing Together: The Arts and Education.* Arlington, Va.: American Association of School Administrators, 1985.

Business and Industry . . . Partners in Education. Arlington, Va.: American Association of School Administrators, 1985.

Cetron, Marvin. *Schools of the Future.* New York: McGraw-Hill, 1985.

Citizens and the Schools . . . Partners in Education. Arlington, Va.: American Association of School Administrators, 1985.

Communications Briefings. 140 S. Broadway, Pitman, N.J. 08071. Monthly newsletter.

Journal of Educational Communication. Publication of the Education Communications Center, Camp Hill, Pa.

Parents . . . Partners in Education (video program). Arlington, Va.: American Association of School Administrators, 1983.

Parents . . . Partners in Education. Arlington, Va.: American Association of School Administrators, 1982. (Also available in Spanish.)

Public Education: A Sound Investment in America (video program). Arlington, Va.: American Association of School Administrators, 1985.

Public Opinion. Washington, D.C.: American Enterprise Institute. Quarterly journal.

Public Relations News. 127 E. 80th St., New York, N.Y. 10021. Weekly newsletter.

Public Relations Quarterly. College Park, Pa. Quarterly journal.

PR Reporter. Dudley House, P.O. Box 600, Exeter, N.H. 03833. Weekly newsletter.

Selecting the Administrative Team. Arlington, Va.: American Association of School Administrators, 1981.

Social Science Monitor. College Park, Md. Monthly newsletter.

Spady, William; and Marx, Gary. *Excellence in our Schools ... Making It Happen*. Arlington, Va.: American Association of School Administrators, 1984.

The Race We Dare Not Lose (slide-tape program). Arlington, Va.: American Association of School Administrators, 1983.

The Ragan Report. 407 S. Dearborn St., Chicago, Ill. 60605. Weekly newsletter.

OTHER RESOURCES

In addition, a variety of special reports, booklets, and monographs are available from national and state associations. To learn what is available, contact the associations. Here are some:

American Association of School Administrators, 1801 N. Moore St., Arlington, Va. 22209-9988. (Publishes *The School Administrator* magazine and various other publications that relate to public relations.)

Education Press Association, Bozorth Hall, Glassboro State College, Glassboro, N.J. 08028.

International Association of Business Communicators, Suite 940, 870 Market St., San Francisco, Calif. 94102. (Publishes *Communications World* magazine.)

National Association of Elementary School Principals, 1920 Association Drive, Reston, Va. 22091.

National Association of Secondary School Principals, 1904 Association Drive, Reston, Va. 22091.

National Community Education Association, 119 N. Payne Street, Alexandria, Va. 22314

National PTA, 700 N. Rush Street, Chicago, Ill. 60611

National School Volunteer Program, 300 N. Washington Street, Alexandria, Va. 22314

National School Boards Association, 1680 Duke St., Alexandria, Va. 22314.

National School Public Relations Association, 1501 Lee Highway, Arlington, Va. 22209. (Publishes *NSPRA Impact, It Starts in the Classroom*, other publications.)

Public Relations Society of America, 845 Third Ave., New York, N.Y. 10022. (Publishes *Public Relations Journal*.)

Women in Communications Inc., Box 9561, Austin, Texas 78766.

Acknowledgments

The American Association of School Administrators (AASA) expresses its appreciation to all who were involved in producing *Public Relations for Administrators*.

Authors Don Bagin, Donald Ferguson, and Gary Marx drew from their public relations knowledge and skills gained both inside and outside education to develop the format for this book and to write and edit copy.

Other public relations professionals who made important contributions to *Public Relations for Administrators* included: Joseph Rowson, who prepared information on nonverbal communication, group dynamics, and interpersonal communication; Joanie Flatt, who prepared information on involving the community and made important additions to chapters devoted to working with the media and publications; Phil Toman, who developed initial copy for the news media chapter; Scott Tilden, who provided valuable information on developing audiovisual programs; Clem Cleveland, who contributed initial thinking and copy for the technology chapter; and John Wherry and Richard Bagin of the National School Public Relations Association (NSPRA) for information on evaluating public relations programs in schools.

Several members of the AASA staff contributed to this publication. Joseph Scherer, associate executive director for the Office of Government Relations, reviewed the chapter on working with government officials. Communications Assistant Nancy Platzer, Unit Coordinator Karen Ellzey, and Managing Editor Joanne Kaldy provided frequent advice, editing, rewriting, and production assistance. AASA Publications Manager Anne Dees served as primary editor, made key additions to the technology chapter, contributed valuable advice, and managed production.

The AASA Foundation Fund provided partial funding to make the project possible. The American Association of School Administrators, the authors and contributors, and the Board of Trustees of the Foundation Fund extend their appreciation to the educational leaders who will ultimately make use of the information in this publication to support better education for students.

About the Authors

Don Bagin is a professor/communications coordinator in the graduate program in school public relations at Glassboro State College in New Jersey. He is an author of *The School & Community Relations*, published by Prentice Hall, and other timely publications devoted to school public relations. Bagin is a frequent speaker and workshop leader and has served as coordinator of the annual National School Public Relations Association publications contest for a number of years. He is a former NSPRA president.

Donald Ferguson is vice president of ENTERCOM, a Denver-based public relations firm. He served for a number of years as public relations director for the Lincoln, Nebraska, public schools. Ferguson has served as director of academies for the National School Boards Association and as a public relations executive for AMAX, a large international mining firm. He has taught journalism courses, is author of a journalism textbook, and was an editor with a daily newspaper. Ferguson continues his work with schools and is a frequent speaker and workshop leader. He is an authority on issues management.

Gary Marx is an associate executive director of the American Association of School Administrators in Arlington, Virginia. Prior to joining AASA, he served as executive director of communications for the Jefferson County public schools in Colorado and the Westside Community schools in Omaha, Nebraska. Marx has spoken at or conducted many workshops on effective school public relations. He served for many years as a broadcaster and has owned a radio station. He is the author of several books and numerous articles on effective communication and has taught communications courses.